Panzer Colors II

**Markings of the German Army
Panzer Forces 1939-45**

631

by Bruce Culver
illustrated by Don Greer

squadron/signal publications

PUBLISHED 1978 by SQUADRON/SIGNAL
PUBLICATIONS, INC.
3461 E. TEN MILE ROAD, WARREN, MICHI-
GAN 48091

ISBN 0-89747-069-9

A Steyr 640, Kfz 31 ambulance of 1. Panzer Division, seen during the opening phase of *Barbarossa.* **It has the usual red and white ambulance markings, plus the division's 1941 yellow inverted "Y" sign and a tactical sign. This vehicle is attached to the HQ staff company of a motorized antitank battalion. (National Archives)**

Acknowledgements

Like most products of months of research and consultation, this book is the result of help from many individuals and organizations. Many of them gave unstintingly of their time and effort to answer questions, and provided published material and personal research data to add to the material being examined. The extent to which this book is more accurate and complete than those previously available is to a very great degree the direct result of their labors and cooperation.

In the United States and Canada, several people helped directly and indirectly with both the preliminary and final research. Several of these speak and write fluent German, which, because I do not, proved to be invaluable to the research effort.

Jon Randolph searched through thousands of published photographs in hundreds of books and magazines to construct a comprehensive listing of known or probable German divisional signs, which was an excellent starting point for determining what more research was needed. Tom McGuirl provided translation services, and the generous use of his collection of wartime German publications, including "Signal" and "Die Wehrmacht", as well as suggestions for writing to the German veterans' groups with requests for information. Tom Jentz gave me a great deal of assistance in going over and captioning many of the photos used in this book, and in letters and conversations gave me many items from his own research work in the captured German documents held in the U.S. National Archives, and correspondence with German veterans. Dave List in England generously provided several British intelligence reports and translations of captured German documents. Steve Zaloga also contributed some captured German material, which proved very useful in documenting German losses in Poland.

In published material, Armin L. Sohns wrote several articles for "AFV-News" on German markings which proved to be excellent references for the relevant sections in this book, and several other articles appeared in "AFV-News" which were very helpful in writing this volume and the one to follow. James Steuard wrote a number of articles in "AFV-G2" covering the small unit organization of German armored formations, and articles dealing with German markings, that provided material on other units. There were also many helpful people in the Modern Military Documents and Audio-Visual sections of the U.S. National Archives. Richard Law's fine book on the D.A.K. provided excellent references on German pennants and flags.

It is the German veterans, of course, who could contribute first hand information to this research. It should be noted that many Germans are reluctant to talk about the war years, especially to people from the Allied nations that won the conflict. It is understandable that such reluctance would exist, especially since so many myths and misconceptions have been printed about German military units—often repeatedly—that many Germans simply have given up trying to answer questions. The tragedy of all this is that history is lost to future generations. So it is extremely fortunate that some German veterans' organizations have taken the time to assist in this research. They responded to the inquiries with published and original materials which have added considerably to the available information on the subject of German markings and history. They have supplied enough data to complete this book. The historical material not used here will be preserved for the historical record and used in future volumes. In some cases, markings have been lost, even with attempts to preserve material, simply because markings were not as important to most officers and men as food and fuel. Nonetheless, many units and individuals were able to provide material, and this book is vastly more complete because of their efforts.

I wish to thank the following, who wrote to me and assisted in this work:

General der Panzertruppe a.D. Walter K. Nehring	- 19. Pzkorps (Pzkps Guderian, 1940) and 18. PD
Dr. jur. Rolf Hinze	- Panzer Artillerie Regiment 19, 19. Panzer Division
Major a.D. Rolf Bering	- 6. Panzer Division
Brigadegeneral a.D. Horst Scheibert	- 6. Panzer Division
Claus D. Berwald	- 23. Panzer Division
General der Panzertruppe a.D. Hasso von Manteuffel	- 7. Panzer Division
Georg Heymer	- Panzer Regiment 35, 4. Panzer Division
Brigadegeneral Freiherr von Rodde	- 3. Panzer Division

Veterans of **Panzer Regiment 8, 15. PD D.A.K.**, as well as veterans of **Panzer Regiments 1, 2** and **18** (**1.** and **18. PD**) - via Rolf Stoves.
Veterans of the **2. Panzer Division** (Wien Division)

I wish to thank also Heinrich Nolte of the **18. Panzergrenadier Division**, and Alfred Ottle of **sJ Panzer Korps "Hermann Göring"** for their kind assistance. Another volume in this series will deal with other German formations not covered here, including these units.

In addition to these veterans and organizations, three stand out for having given extra effort to assist me. Rittmeister a.D. H. - R. Klippert of **24. Panzer Division** provided a complete set of organization charts for his division from its inception as the **1. Kavallerie Division** in 1940 to the last table of organization in 1945. Oberst a.D. Helmut Ritgen of **Panzer Lehr Division** also provided research material, detailed letters, photographs of **Panzer Lehr Division** tanks, and most generously loaned me his own copy of the book "Taktische Zeichen des Heeres" (Tactical Signs of the Army) which was the primary source for tactical markings in the German Army from 1939-42.

Finally, but certainly not least, was Oberstlt a.D. Rolf O.G. Stoves, of **1. Panzer Division** and **21. Panzer Division** (DAK), who served in the post-war Bundeswehr and has been a military historian for a number of years, lecturing at German Army training establishments including the armor training school (Panzertruppenschule) at Munsterlager. Oberstlt. Stoves not only wrote many voluminous and detailed letters in answer to my questions, but also sent me historical material covering or listing almost every German armored unit that existed during World War II. In addition to concise histories of the WW 2 Panzer Divisions, Oberstlt. Stoves provided listings of markings from several sources, and a complete listing of virtually all Army (Heeres) Panzer units, from divisions to independent regiments and battalions.

Without Rolf Stoves' very generous and complete assistance, this book could not have been written in its present form and content. His concern, as mine, has been to have this book represent the most accurate accounting of WW 2 German military markings—a part of the history of that war—and it is our belief that, within the confines of the format of this work, it is the best source on German military markings currently available. I wish to thank him very much for his most generous cooperation.

Bruce Culver
December, 1977

Introduction

Military markings, in the basic sense of providing identification in battle, can be traced back to Neolithic man. Tribes and village clans would often paint themselves with distinctive patterns of "warpaint". In some other cases, tattoos or scars were used to mark members of a clan or tribe. These were permanent markings that usually had religious or mystical ritual meanings, and were not solely for use in warfare. Later in history, as armies became more organized in the specialty of military action for conquest or defense, flags, banners, and standards came into use to rally troops in the field and identify the positions of commanders. While elite troops (many of them professional soldiers hired and equipped by rulers or nobles) often wore standard uniforms which helped units stay together, the use of auxiliaries (who usually wore a variety of clothing) made the use of flags imperative. Most military transport was by horse drawn wagons, and these were sometimes, during the Middle ages, hung with regimental flags and used as rallying points. These can be considered the first modern military markings.

World War I saw the first widespread use of national symbols, on aircraft and, in some cases, on armored vehicles. Unit symbols, such as the French system of playing card signs, were used to denote smaller organizations (regiments, battalions, companies, or platoons). Occasionally, vehicles carried individual identifying numbers within these units.

By the beginning of World War II, most nations had developed systems of symbols for their military vehicles and equipment. Modern military markings were developed with the conflicting goals of identifying units to friendly troops while denying this information to the enemy.

The United States adopted a system of markings that displayed the unit numbers (with letter or symbol designators) on all vehicles. This was easy to read, but had the disadvantage that the markings for the major and sub units often had to be removed in forward areas for security reasons. The British used a coded system utilizing divisional signs or emblems and colored square/number combinations to denote units within the division. By periodically changing the colors or numbers, it was possible to conceal the true identity and make-up of a division. This system worked well.

Germany, in the interwar period, used few markings and those were based on the World War I system. With the rise to power of the *NSDAP* (Nazi party) and Hitler's rejection of the Treaty of Versailles, the German military organizations (already having several years of clandestine experience in development and planning) were brought into the open. In the mid- and late 1930s, Germany increased her military preparations, and part of those preparations was the development of a system of markings to denote unit and sub-unit identity and organization.

There were ten markings categories that could be applied to German military vehicles, though most never carried all of these: national symbols, divisional symbols, tactical signs, vehicle numbers, license plates, service and maintenance markings, rank pennants or flags, award shields or crests, victory markings, and vehicle markings. Many vehicles, however, did carry a good number of these markings.

Contrary to what many have believed about wartime German markings, there was a good deal of variation in many of the systems and markings actually used. In many cases, variations resulted from a shortage of proper application stencils or guidebooks, or because the personnel marking the vehicles were unfamiliar with the correct symbols and substituted those they thought to be correct. In other cases, unit morale and background often led to variations—there were instances in which units continued to use "old" or unofficial markings in place of the official symbols approved by OKW. If a division or regiment—or even a company— had a superior fighting record, such deviations were usually tolerated to maintain morale, as long as their meaning was clear to the local troops. In addition, many divisions were ordered to alter or replace their normal insignia to disguise troop movements, especially before major offensives. Some of these "temporary" changes became permanent. Others were used for a few weeks or months and then replaced. A few units received new signs during the buildup for *Barbarossa* (during the expansion of the *Panzer Divisions*) but reverted to their old signs for morale reasons—some in fact never completely switched to the new symbols in the first place!

Besides variations in the symbols and emblems, there also were changes in the colors used. Many divisional signs were painted in "unofficial" colors, others were painted in a variety of colors, and many were painted in different colors for different camouflage schemes. On relatively rare occasions, even the *Balkenkreuz* national symbol was painted in unofficial colors or an unusual style. Vehicle numbers were often painted in different colors, sometimes because of camouflage colors, other times because they were too prominent or not prominent enough.

German military markings were modified during the war, and many variations existed. The tables of organization of all German formations changed several times—the *Panzer Divisions* an average of once a year. Old units were abolished or changed and new ones formed. New weapons entered service, old ones retired, and different symbols were introduced to cover these changes. There were alterations based on combat or evaluation reports, and in the normal course of military review. Occasionally, old affiliations were changed, as in the change in many reconnaissance units in 1943, when they abandoned the old cavalry nomenclature and organization. Many vehicles on short term or temporary assignments to another unit often carried partial or complete signs for both. Finally, the well-documented shortages—and lack of time in many situations— often resulted in vehicles that carried virtually no markings, even when security regulations allowed them.

This book will cover the marking practices of the German Army (*Heere*) Panzer Divisions from the period 1939-45. Early German vehicles carried few markings apart from temporary maneuvers insignia. It was the start of World War II in 1939 that lent the impetus to the use of tactical markings. In any discussion of these markings, it is best to consider the early war and later war as separate periods. The early war period was from 1939-40 (the Polish and Western campaigns), the later war period being from 1941-45 (*Barbarossa* to Berlin). These coincide with the major changes in the divisional signs and the first big revision in the formations of most Panzer Divisions.

It is extremely unlikely that the whole story of World War II German military markings will ever be known. Many units existed for such a short time that it is doubtful that any markings were assigned, much less used. Many formations were sufficiently destroyed or crippled in action that little information remains, as few survivors were left to maintain a history of the units. The great destruction of German cities and archives in the last months of the war also took its toll of historical material—for example, all records of the **4. Panzer Division (Pz Rgt 35)** were lost during the Battle of Berlin, and the photo archives of *Der Adler* were reported destroyed in a bombing raid. Also many historical records were destroyed by German military authorities at the end of the war. In other cases, memories have faded—markings were usually not uppermost in the mind of the average soldier—and only a few poorly labeled (or unexplained) photographs exist to remind us of the great variations that did exist within the well-documented standard practices seen elsewhere.

This PzKpfw I ausf A seen during training carries a checkerboard turret marking that indicated the company headquarters platoon. This marking was not used for long, as the color coding of companies and platoons was not made a standard practice, and the adoption of command unit numbers superceded this design.

PzKpfw Is ausf A seen during maneuvers. They are using the old *Reichswehr* camouflage colors, and carry no national insignia. The vehicle marking here is in white. The two dark bands indicate the second platoon of a company. (Bundesarchiv)

A public display of armor early in the Third Reich, probably 1935. The lead tank's pennant carries the *Totenkopf* (Death's Head), the symbol of all tank troops *(Panzertruppen)*. The lead tank also seems to have the *Reichswehr* gray and brown scheme.

National Insignia

The German national insignia, the *Balkenkreuz*, was first seen on military vehicles during the campaign in Poland, 1939. It was felt that there was a need for a distinctive marking to differentiate German combat vehicles from those of the enemy, and to provide proper identification to Luftwaffe pilots. The *Balkenkreuz* was to be applied only to armored combat vehicles, and though there were occasional exceptions, during World War II, German softskins did not carry this national sign. In forward areas, captured enemy cars and trucks—especially those with distinctive silhouettes—were painted with the *Balkenkreuz* to identify them to German troops. A few vehicles had swastikas applied to them as unofficial national insignia, often in fairly crude hand-painted versions.

The *Balkenkreuz* underwent several changes during the war. The first design, used at the start of the Polish campaign, was a prominent all-white cross. Occasionally, this was not painted directly on the vehicles, but applied as a cutout metal plate, often over cooling grills, shutters, or hatches that were open at times. The Germans soon realized that the white *Balkenkreuz* was too prominent. More tanks were being hit by Polish antitank guns than had been anticipated: the cross made an excellent aiming point. The first reaction by field troops was to cover the crosses with mud. Shortly, however, a more permanent solution was found: the centers of all crosses were overpainted in the deep yellow used for divisional insignia. Often a narrow border of white remained, but many crosses were painted completely yellow. Many German tanks in Poland were thus fairly colorful, with dark gray paint and a mix of yellow and white markings.

The Polish experience led to the development of an acceptable national cross marking. The final design was an open cross, similar to that used by the Luftwaffe, painted in white on the dark gray vehicles. The center of the cross was to be left in the dark gray vehicle color, and no black outer borders were authorized. As individual units and crews were responsible for repainting the insignia, there were numerous variations, and crosses with black centers and/or black outer borders were seen.

Variations in the style of the crosses resulted from several factors. Some vehicles simply had dark gray (occasionally black) lines painted across the centers of the Polish white crosses. Since most combat vehicles in Poland ended up with yellow crosses, the insignia were usually completely repainted. Usually, correct stencils were available, but where they were not used, variations in proportions could be found. Repaired vehicles were generally repainted at the factories, and Germany's increased production efforts added still more vehicles during the "Phoney War" period, 1939-40. Thus, by the beginning of the campaign against France and the Low Countries in the spring of 1940, most German combat vehicles carried the correct style *Balkenkreuz*. Various sizes were in use, but a common size used on *PzKpfw III's* and *IV's* was about 10" (25 cm) high. This all-white outline cross was retained on dark gray combat vehicles until the change to dark yellow in 1943.

The campaign in North Africa, begun in February 1941, produced another change in the *Balkenkreuz*. The adoption of yellow-brown camouflage made the white outline crosses hard to see. As a result, the centers were filled in with black paint to improve the contrast. The proportions were the same as before, and the black and white cross was virtually identical to the cross used on German fighter fuselages. There were a number of variations, among these were long narrow crosses similar to some of the filled-in "Polish" crosses, and various handpainted alterations of the standard cross.

It was also in Africa that the problem of identifying captured enemy equipment first appeared, as earlier campaigns had not involved widespread use of captured vehicles. The shortage of German transport and the superior desert performance of British trucks led to the use of many Allied vehicles in German units. Many captured vehicles had distinctive shapes and thus were marked with prominent crosses to prevent their being fired on accidentally by friendly troops. These crosses were oversize, often covering the entire door of a truck or car—some of them apparently resulted from merely extending the arms of the standard AFV *Balkenkreuz*. Others were completely handpainted and differed considerably. In Tunisia, captured Allied vehicles were usually marked in bold crosses, usually black with white borders, though some with reversed colors (white with black borders) were seen. Some vehicles, re-marked in a hurry, had crude crosses or swastikas handpainted on the top and sides, often in white.

The adoption of dark yellow paint as the *einheits* color in February 1943 led to the adoption of the black and white *Balkenkreuz* for all vehicles so marked. This was identical to the African version, and the sizes also remained the same, generally 8" (20 cm) to 10" (25 cm) high. Usually, stencils were used to apply the crosses, generally by tracing the border through the stencil and handpainting the marking or by spraying through the stencil to produce the complete shape. The rough zimmerit paste used on many vehicles from 1943-44 resulted in rough, uneven crosses and other markings with either the spraying or handpainting methods.

It should be noted that while the "official" standard *Balkenkreuz* was black with white borders and no black outer borders, there were variations because of the large number of vehicles that had to be repainted periodically and re-marked. Among the variations seen were crosses with the black outer borders, crosses in white with black borders, outline crosses in black or white, and crosses with unofficial colors—such as red—used for the white outline borders. In addition, some factory markings appear to have been non-standard. As an example, all the *Opel Maultier* armored halftracks, especially the version with the *15 cm Panzerwerfer 42* rocket launcher, used a narrow cross with long arms very similar to some

This Adler Kfz 13 MG carrier of a reconnaissance battalion in Poland shows the early white crosses used to identify German combat vehicles. These markings have been painted on, even over the front cooling louvers. All these vehicles have been given names. (Bundesarchiv)

non-standard crosses seen in France and North Africa. This could have been a deliberate choice of style, or simply what someone in the assembly plant thought would be satisfactory.

Some captured vehicles—especially Russian equipment on the Eastern front—were officially marked with oversize crosses because of the problems of proper identification. Other vehicles had normal size *Balkenkreuz* markings, but carried many more than German vehicles would. Vehicles captured in large numbers were often introduced into service as standard vehicle types, and were marked as though they were of German manufacture, as was done with the hundreds of British trucks captured in France, 1940. These received German military nomenclature, *Notek* lights, license plates and paint schemes, plus standard German military softskin markings where applicable.

The second type of national insignia was the national flag—the black swastika in a white disc on a red field which was draped or tied over an available upper surface of a vehicle to serve as an air recognition sign for *Luftwaffe* pilots. The problem of identifying friendly troops and vehicles from the air has always been serious, and every army has had the experience of being attacked by its own air force. The large, easily seen German flag was an excellent air recognition sign, and was widely used wherever the *Luftwaffe* had established air superiority. As the war progressed, and the Allies gained air superiority on most fronts, the use of the national flag became less frequent and was rare during the last years of the war. In those cases where it was used at all, there usually were provisions for removing or covering the flag quickly when enemy aircraft were sighted.

Also used at various times were painted air recognition signs on German vehicles. Generally, these appear to have been either white crosses,, white bands, or long rectangles. This marking was used in the 1939-1940 campaigns and in North Africa, and may have been used elsewhere, too. In North Africa, Italian combat equipment was often marked with white crosses on upper surfaces, such as a turret roof or bow plate, since it was usually operated in close cooperation with German units.

One bizarre—and limited—example of air recognition signs on German vehicles was the use of standard U.S. colored air recognition I.D. panels on the disguised *Panthers* (M10s) and *StuG. III*'s of *Panzer Brigade 150* during the 1944 Ardennes Offensive. These vehicles were intended to masquerade as U.S. armor to confuse and mislead American troops. Though ultimately unsuccessful, the deception was planned well enough to involve use of captured U.S. I.D. panels.

This PzKpfw IV ausf A in Poland shows the white cross and number, and the very high visibility of these markings. Polish antitank gunners found these bold markings to be excellent aiming points, and only the PzKpfw IV among German armor had 30 mm of frontal armor.

Balkankreuz Variations

Solid White   Yellow w/White Outline   Solid Yellow

This SdKfz 247 command vehicle has its white crosses added on metal plates attached to the body. This was done on a number of vehicles in the Polish campaign. Note the triangular battalion pennant on the right side, and the open rectangular frame on the left. (Bundesarchiv)

This photograph is a graphic example of the difference in visibility between the original white markings at right and the mud-smeared markings at left. This was a temporary expedient, but was effective. These are both PzKpfw IVs ausf A. (Bundesarchiv)

Once the Germans realized the crosses were too prominent, the crews quickly covered them with mud, as seen on these PzKpfw Is. Thinner smears of mud have been used to smudge the turret numbers, but the crosses have been nearly completely covered. (Bundesarchiv)

These tanks, two PzKpfw Is and a PzKpfw II, show crosses repainted in yellow with white borders retained. The PzKpfw II cross is bolder because the white borders are wider and the central yellow narrower. The turret numbers are yellow on these vehicles. (Bundesarchiv)

A PzKpfw I ausf B with a very cautious crew, seen in Poland. The crosses have been repainted in yellow with white borders, and then covered with a coating of mud. Again note the all-yellow numbers, a relatively common marking. (Bundesarchiv)

This PzKpfw II has an unusual variation of the overpainted cross. This marking has been filled in with dark gray in place of the usual yellow. (Bundesarchiv)

Two PzKpfw IIs in Poland carry markings completely over-painted in yellow. They are very low in contrast, and probably were difficult to see at any distance. This is why many crosses were left with white borders. Some units also left tank numbers in white as the all yellow numbers were hard to see under some conditions. (Bundesarchiv)

A PzKpfw II of *PzAufkl Abt 2* (Recon Battalion) of 12. Panzer Division has the standard white outline cross used from 1940-43. The division sign is yellow and on the turret rear is the tank number "A" (large) "94" (smaller), also in yellow. Note the rear mounted discharge tubes for firing smoke shells. (Bundesarchiv)

A PzKpfw II of 7. Panzer Division in France carries the new style cross of the narrow type. The appearance of black around and in the cross is caused by brand new dark gray paint used to paint over the old Polish campaign crosses. Note the white air recognition band painted across the engine deck. (Bundesarchiv)

A SdKfz 231 armored car in southern France, 1942, shows the wider variation of the open white cross. Note the tire pressure notations above each wheel. (Bundesarchiv)

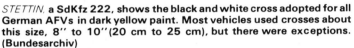

STETTIN, a SdKfz 222, shows the black and white cross adopted for all German AFVs in dark yellow paint. Most vehicles used crosses about this size, 8'' to 10'' (20 cm to 25 cm), but there were exceptions. (Bundesarchiv)

Apparently all Opel *Maultier* armored halftracks used this nonstandard cross in which the center black strokes were the same width as the white borders. ''G'', in black and white, is the vehicle identification letter. The white border lines for night driving were used even on many dark yellow vehicles. (Bundesarchiv)

This Panther ausf A in Russia shows the slight roughened effect of *zimmerit* on the cross. The turret numbers are white with thin black outlines. (Bundesarchiv)

This knocked out SdKfz 251 ausf D has unusual crosses, made by using the standard stencils but with open centers. Such variations were the result of crew preferences in most cases. Note the 4-digit number, indicating a regiment or battalion headquarters vehicle. (Public Archives of Canada)

This photo of a captured T-34/76 model 43 being painted shows how the crosses were applied. The stencil is being traced with chalk and the cross center will be handpainted in black, then the white borders will be added. This cross is vastly oversize to reduce the danger of German troops firing on this tank because of its distinctive shape. (Bundesarchiv)

The only ''national'' marking on this captured Canadian Ford CMP truck in Greece is the ''WH'' notation on the fender. Serviceable captured vehicles were often used immediately, before there was time to mark them properly. (Bundesarchiv)

This 3-ton Canadian CMP truck has been thoroughly repainted and marked. Note the number of large crosses and the white air recognition band across the top of the engine compartment. The license number has been painted on the bumper in black only. The windshield has also been partially painted to reduce glare from reflected sunlight. (Bundesarchiv)

A Willys MB jeep captured in Tunisia displays very crude swastikas, a rather unusual marking even for captured softskins. Note the blue drab serial number on the side of the hood. This was a US low visibility marking. (Bundesarchiv)

British trucks, like this 1/2 ton Canadian Dodge 4 x 4 radio truck, generally had very good desert performance and were highly prized by the DAK. This vehicle retains its British tan paint scheme, very recent by the look of the painted tires. The new owners have added a crude cross for recognition purposes. (Bundesarchiv)

A captured US M8 armored car retains its olive drab color scheme but has a large cross in white, the center bands being left O.D. The fenders have been removed which alters the appearance of this vehicle a good deal. (Bundesarchiv)

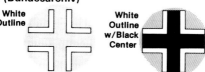

White Outline

White Outline w/Black Center

The Germans captured thousands of Russian vehicles including many of these Komsomoletz STZ-3 tractors. Though many vehicles were used in Russian green, this example has been repainted dark gray. These crosses are much narrower than usual, but many of these tractors had similar crosses.

Occasionally, captured vehicles were simply marked with a large number of normal size crosses. This Sherman V "Firefly" has also had some olive-green or red-brown sprayed over the khaki paint scheme. (Bundesarchiv)

A Horch Kfz 17, seen bogged down in a watery ditch in North Africa, shows clearly the good contrast provided by the colors of the national flag. This vehicle still has the temporary coating of mud over dark gray. (Bundesarchiv)

This PzKpfw III seen in Poland has a swastika as an air recognition sign. This was fairly unusual, but not unknown. The front cross was retouched in the original print. (Steve Zaloga)

This PzKpfw IV ausf D of 1. Panzer Division has had a white cross painted on the turret roof as an air recognition sign. Many vehicles, especially softskins, had white bands painted across the engine compartments for the same purpose. (Bundesarchiv)

Vehicle Number

Much of the credit for the German successes in the early years of the war, often against technically superior tanks, is due to the superior training and better employment of German armor in the classic maneuvers of breakthrough, encirclement, and exploitation. German tanks, even when out-gunned and facing heavily armored French and British tanks in the 1940 campaign, were better suited for the needs of armored warfare, as the duties of the crew were separated into different functions for each member, and the vehicle design did not require one man to do too many jobs at once.

Part of the superiority in German tactics was the training in formation movement and assault. As part of this training, the Germans found that it was helpful to be able to identify each vehicle so that a company or platoon commander could direct his vehicles more efficiently. In time, most German armored vehicles, particularly tanks, came to use individual numbers and/or letter designators to indicate their positions in a formation. Many armored personnel carriers, armored cars, and self-propelled weapons carried these markings too.

Some tanks carried painted numbers on their turrets before the war, but these were replaced by the use of small rhomboid-shaped metal plates which displayed the vehicle number. The plates were detachable, and if a vehicle had to be taken out of service, the crew removed the number plates and transferred them to a substitute vehicle, which then adopted the same number. This proved to be a very useful procedure during training, and was widely used before the war.

Early Panzer Divisions were quite large, numbering up to 400 tanks in a Panzer Brigade, which contained two Panzer Regiments. Each Panzer Regiment had two battalions (Abteilung), and these contained either two light tank companies and one medium company, or three light companies and one medium company. A company contained three or four platoons, and a platoon had three to five tanks, depending on the type of vehicle and formation organization.

The numbering system chosen was very simple: a three digit number was painted on the rhomboid plate to indicate the tank's exact position within the division. The first numeral indicated the company, the second the platoon (zug) within the company, and the third the vehicle within the platoon. Thus 332 meant: 3rd company, 3rd platoon, 2nd tank in the platoon. This was the standard numbering system used throughout the war.

Command vehicles carried a modified system based on the above. Regimental staff vehicles were marked with an R prefix, and battalion command tanks carried a Roman numeral prefix corresponding to the number of the battalion within the regiment: I, II, or III. R01 was the tank of the regimental commander, R02 the regimental AD (assistant to the commander, "executive officer"), R03 was the regimental signals officer, and higher numbers designated other regimental officers and the light tanks of the regimental HQ reconnaissance platoon. Some regiments used non-standard number systems: R00 being the commander's command tank— if R00 was damaged, R01 became the regimental command vehicle. In most regiments, R02 was the spare, and the regimental AD was to take another vehicle if the commander had to use R02.

Battalion command vehicles used a similar system, substituting the Roman numeral of the battalion for the regimental R. Thus I01 was the tank of the commander of the first battalion of a panzer regiment. II01 was used by the commander of the second battalion, and III01 was for the commander of the third. In the first battalion, I02 was the AD, I03 was the signals officer, and I04 usually the ordnance officer. Again, I02 was considered the spare tank for the battalion commander and the AD was to take another vehicle if the battallion CO had to take over I02. This was because usually only a few vehicles, R01—R03, or I01—I03, had command radios. The II and III battalions followed the same numbering scheme, and the higher numbers again referred to other battalion officers and the light tanks of the battalion HQ reconnaissance platoon.

Some divisions used a very different system of marking their regimental staff vehicles. Instead of using R designators—which would draw attention to the regimental staff—they used false "company" numbers. This was especially true later in the war when most divisions had one regiment with two battalions of tanks. If the regiment had 8 companies in two battalions, the regimental tanks sometimes carried 901, 902, 903, etc. Other units used 0 numerals: 001, 002, 003, 014, etc. A few regiments had a 9th company of Tiger tanks, and in this case, the regimental vehicles would carry a 10th company marking: 1001, 1002, 1003, 1012, etc. It has been reported that the 500 series was occasionally reserved for regimental or battalion staff vehicles, but this is not confirmed. And as every Panzer Regiment had a 5th company, the use of 500 numbers for regimental or battalion staff vehicles would have been confusing. Markings in the high 500 series (562 being one example seen) may, however, indicate command tanks.

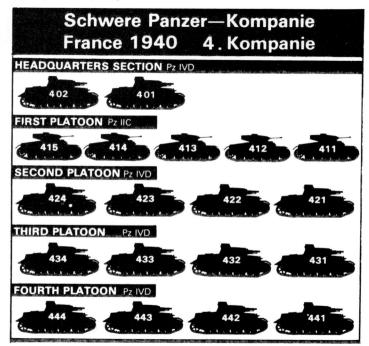

In April 1944, the Inspector General of armored troops (*Panzertruppen*) issued an order, to take effect by 15 June 1944, that standardized this previously "unofficial" coding system for numbering regimental and battalion headquarters and command vehicles. The order also directed the use of the 3-digit numbering system for all APCs (armored Halftracks) in *Panzergrenadier Regiments* and armored reconnaissance battalions, and observation vehicles. Thus, some semblance of uniformity was introduced and, in theory, all units in a *Panzer Division* were to use the same numbering system.

The numbers and letters used for regiment and battalion command units were to be completely altered. In place of the **R** or **I** and **II** designators for their vehicles, regiment and battalion commands were to choose 2-digit code numbers to identify the vehicles in the command formations. Because the number of companies in the division support units could go into two digits (**11, 14,** etc.) all regiment and battalion codes were to be chosen at random from numbers above **20**. Regrettably, at present there are no available records as to the regiments and battalions that used these coded numbers, or the numbers used by each unit.

In spite of the issuing of this general order, it is obvious from photographic evidence that a number of divisions did not follow this order, or did not follow it completely. As was the case with divisional and personal insignia and emblems, some divisions preferred to retain their traditional markings, or did not always add the full range of new numbers to all their APCs or self-propelled guns and artillery. Nonetheless, this order does explain the existence of higher 4-digit numbers found on many German vehicles in 1944-45.

Within the companies, the commander's tank was usually numbered **01**, as: **301, 501, 601,** etc., but in some cases, it was **300, 500, 800,** etc. The second tank was the spare command tank, normally operated by the company *AD*, or second in command, and turned over to the CO if his first tank was disabled.

The above system was the basic marking scheme for designating vehicle positions. The numbers changed slightly with the change in formation organization. The *Panzer Brigade* with two regiments (4 battalions) gave way to a single regiment of three, then two, battalions, and the battalions had generally 4 companies during the middle period of the war. The early light tank platoons usually had 5 tanks, but the standard mid-war platoon usually had 4 tanks, though 5 tank platoons existed. Thus, a three platoon company had 14 (or 17) tanks: two in the staff section, and 4 (or 5) tanks in each of the three platoons. This was used for all types of German tanks from the *PzKpfw III* to the *Tiger II* (King Tiger).

All German tanks were assigned these 3-digit numbers, and the vehicles were generally referred to by their numbers: "**431** needs an oil change"; "**324**, enemy infantry 200 meters to your left", etc. A number of units, however, did not paint the full numbers on the vehicles, and this has caused a great deal of confusion. Two alternate systems were encountered: one-digit numbers and two-digit numbers. The one-digit system referred to the company the tank was in; the two-digit number referred to the platoon and vehicle number. Thus **7** or **5** referred to the 7th or 5th companies, but made no reference to the platoon or vehicle. **23, 14,** or **33** referred (in order) to: 3rd tank of the 2nd platoon, 4th tank of the 1st platoon, and 3rd tank of the 3rd platoon, but made no mention of the company number. These systems seem to have been consistent, and thus the numbers can be read as straight identification of the company, or the platoon and vehicle, in most cases.

One other deviation from the standard numbering system was used. This was a consecutive numbering sequence in which all tanks in a company were numbered without regard to platoon or vehicle position: **301—314,** with **306, 309, 310** among the numbers. Obviously, in some cases it is impossible to distinguish between the consecutive and normal 3-digit systems. The consecutive numbering system was not widespread, and the occasional uses of other variations using three numerals can make the deciphering of tank numbers a bit more difficult.

Other vehicle types in the division (or smaller unit) used different designators to mark vehicle positions. Artillery regiments often used letters to denote battalions (or batteries) in the regiment, and many self-propelled guns carried only these single letters. Some assault gun and tank destroyer units used the 3-digit tank number system, and other artillery units used a combination, in which the battalion letter was followed by a two-digit number denoting the battery and gun number, or as a consecutive vehicle number within the battery: **A06** = 6th gun, 1st battalion; **A12** = 2nd gun, 1st battery, 1st battalion. Occasionally, single or double numbers were found on guns. This was simply the use of the numbers without the battalion letter. Some artillery units used the 3-digit system, the first digit indicating the battalion number in place of the more usual letter. Higher numbers (having 4 digits) were usually reserved for support units, such as armored cars, etc. However, the exact sequence of company numbering depended on an individual division's table of organization and the way in which the division staff decided to number their companies.

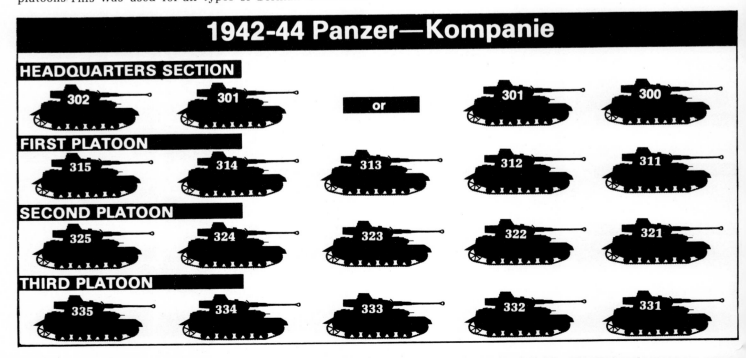

1942-44 Panzer—Kompanie

HEADQUARTERS SECTION

302   301   or   301   300

FIRST PLATOON

315   314   313   312   311

SECOND PLATOON

325   324   323   322   321

THIRD PLATOON

335   334   333   332   331

Application of Numbers

The occasional prewar use of large numbers painted on the vehicles' turret sides had given way to the use of small separate rhomboid-shaped metal plates for carrying the vehicle numbers. These were usually removable and went with the crew if they had to switch to a new tank—in this way, their position in the company was the same, and training was not interrupted to change the company organization when vehicles needed servicing. The plates were usually dark gray with white numbers, but some units used black plates with white numbers. The rhomboid plates were used well into 1941 by several divisions, but it was soon appreciated that in the smoke and dust of battle, they were too small to be seen from very far, thus their combat effectiveness was limited.

By the start of the offensive into Poland, 1939, many *Panzer Divisions* had revived the earlier, limited, practice of painting larger numbers on the sides and rear of their tank turrets. The rhomboid plates were retained, but generally played little part in identifying the vehicles in combat. Almost all the turret numbers used at the start of the Polish campaign were solid white, and stood out extremely well against the dark gray of the vehicles. As it turned out, they (and the solid white crosses) stood out too well, and Polish antitank gunners knocked hundreds of German tanks out of action. The use of solid shot and the superior German recovery efforts meant that almost all of these vehicles were repaired or later remanufactured, but in the field, German losses were much higher than the high command had anticipated—some 800 tanks were knocked out during the entire Polish campaign.

The first reaction by field units was to cover the prominent white crosses with mud, and many units similarly covered the large white numbers. The next alternative was the use of the yellow ochre color used for divisional insignia to paint over the centers of the crosses, and in many cases, the numbers were repainted in yellow. Some vehicles had the numbers repainted smaller in yellow. Others, however, retained the white numbers.

In the "Phoney War" period, 1939-40, some experimentation was done in developing new markings. The use of numbers had been proven effective in action, the problem being to develop numbers that could be seen by German formation commanders yet not be so conspicuous as to serve as an aiming point for enemy gunners. A number of variants were seen during the campaign in France and the Low Countries including numbers on rhomboid plates, white numbers painted somewhat smaller and narrower than in Poland, and open numbers consisting of a white outline with center left in the dark gray of the vehicle, filled in red to contrast better against the gray. There were a variety of styles since each unit prepared its own stencils, and some numbers were painted by hand. There were specified sizes and styles of numbers, but these often were ignored in combat areas.

After the campaign in France was concluded, a major expansion of the *Panzertruppen* took place in preparation for the invasion of Russia. The number of *Panzer Divisions* was doubled and thousands of new men and vehicles had to be welded into effective fighting units. Vehicle numbers were applied as before, occasionally with the use of different colors, such as black centers for numbers. The solid numbers were sometimes painted in colors, and in some cases this appears to have been used as an identification color for companies or platoon. In order, the identifying colors were: white, red, yellow, and blue. Light green was used for a 5th company or sub-unit, and dark green was used for HQ units when colors were used for identification. Obviously, there could be numerous variations, and often one color was used for all vehicles in a *Panzer Regiment,* usually for reasons of optimum visibility (red was popular in North Africa, as black stood out against the tan paint enough to compromise the camouflage in some cases).

Normally, numbers and letters were applied with stencils, either as outlines which were filled in by hand, or as a solid shape. Many numbers, though, were painted by hand, and the size, uniformity, and neatness of application depended entirely on the artistic abilities of the crewman or ordnance workshop crew. This ranged from stencil-like neatness to unspeakable crudity. German tank numbers thus were never standardized more than the exigencies of combat and shortages of time and materials would allow.

These PzKpfw Is seen after the end of the Polish campaign show the small number plates. "I08" denotes a tank of the headquarters reconnaissance platoon of a tank battalion *(Pz Abt).* The crosses are still white since not all units repainted their vehicles' markings in yellow. The first tank also has a barely visible "Death's Head" armor troop symbol. (Bundesarchiv)

Since the small rhomboid plate numbers were not visible in many combat conditions, larger turret numbers were introduced. When these proved too visible in Poland, some units repainted them in yellow as on this PzKpfw I. It was common to find both rhomboid plates and turret numbers.

This PzKpfw III ausf H has fairly neat white numbers, probably done by hand. Note the areas of wet and dried mud on the chassis and hull. The field radio in the foreground was the standard portable field unit, widely used by all services. (Bundesarchiv)

A PzKpfw IV in France, 1940-41, shows the difference in size possible between the rhomboid plate and turret numbers. The latter here are red and white. (Bundesarchiv)

Divisional Signs

Throughout most of World War II, most German military vehicles carried a division identification symbol or emblem. Some of these symbols were chosen by the division, but most of them were issued by **OKW** *(Oberkommando Wehrmacht*-Armed Forces High Command). Such symbols were used to keep the division's identity a secret, and to confuse enemy intelligence as to the exact makeup of a German Army's formations. In practice, of course, many divisions became so well identified by their chosen symbols that any secrecy was lost. Nonetheless, the use of such symbols often contributed to the morale of a division, and despite efforts by **OKW** and **OKH** (Army High Command) "unofficial" symbols were used to improve morale and maintain the historical traditions of the divisions. On this point, divisional signs and emblems can be seen as a modern extension of medieval heraldry.

Before the detailed preparations for the invasion of Poland, some German divisions adopted emblems chosen to represent the units. Sometimes these had to do with the previous history of the division or predecessor units, the area of Germany where the division was recruited, or a part of the history of Germany and its predecessor states. Many of these emblems were very colorful, and some did rival the pageantry of medieval heraldry. Most of the armored divisions adopted somewhat simpler symbols, as in the **1. Panzer Division's** white oakleaf, or **3. Panzer Division's** "Berlin Bear". Photographic evidence shows relatively few divisional symbols used in the Polish campaign, though a three-pointed star tentatively identified as being from the **4. Panzer Division** was used in the Warsaw fighting.

The French campaign in 1940 saw the first widespread use of **OKW** approved divisional signs to identify unit vehicles. Some divisions were given new symbols, perhaps to conceal the troop movements prior to the invasion of France and the Low Countries. Other divisions kept their older symbols or used both the older sign and the new one. **3. Panzer Division** used two signs in 1940: the 1939 OKW sign (an "E"-arms down) and the "Berlin Bear" emblem. Most of the signs used from 1939-40 have been authenticated. The 1940 signs for the **8., 9., and 10. Panzer Divisions** have not been established in photos. The newly discovered sign for **4. Panzer Division** has been confirmed by several captioned photos from the National Archives, very fortunately, as **4. Panzer Division** records were destroyed during the Battle of Berlin, 1945. The traditional source for markings during the war, a British translation of the interrogation of German veterans, has been proven wrong in a number of instances, and the confusion caused by divisional sign changes does not help the situation.

At the end of the campaign in France, preparations got under way for the invasion of England. When this was eventually abandoned, the invasion of Russia *(Barbarossa)* became the primary operation. The early *Panzer Divisions* had been found to be overly large and not well-balanced, as there usually was a preponderance of armor to the available support units. In the late summer and fall of 1940, the structure of the *Panzer Divisions* was changed and the number of divisions was doubled. Instead of a *Panzer Brigade* with (usually) 4 battalions, the new *Panzer Divisions* had a *Panzer Regiment* with 3 battalions. In order to conceal troop movements, a completely new series of divisional symbols was developed by **OKW**, and was to be applied to all *Panzer Division* vehicles. The new signs, though designed for *Barbarossa*, were in fact used for the rest of the war by most of these divisions. Later, as more *Panzer Divisions* were formed in 1942-44, **OKW** often adopted the divisions' chosen symbols as the official signs for reasons of morale, but in 1940-41, the **OKW** signs were more or less arbitrarily assigned, many of them appearing in definite order **(1.-4. PD: 8.-10. PD)**. Some divisions, reluctant to give up their own symbols, marked only a few vehicles in each unit

with the "official" sign, the remainder carrying the old marking. Thus, most vehicles in **1. Panzer Division** retained the white oakleaf while the "official" yellow inverted **"Y"** was painted on lead vehicles. War correspondents and photographers were politely but firmly asked to photograph only the properly marked vehicles so as not to get the division into trouble. After a division or other unit had established a good combat record, such deviations were usually tolerated for morale purposes. Later, in the 1943-45 period, many divisions chose their own symbols, **OKW** attempting to prevent duplication. Even this was unsuccessful. Eight divisions chose the bear as a symbol, and eight other divisions chose variants of the "sunwheel" and swastika.

The divisional insignia for *Panzer Divisions, Panzergrenadier Divisions,* and "Light" Divisions—as well as many motorized Infantry Divisions—were applied in a deep yellow ochre. There were color deviations, caused by changes in camouflage schemes, shortages of paint, or divisional preferences (white oakleaf for **1. Panzer;** white grayhound for **116. Panzer**). The more common colors used were black, red, and white. **15. Panzer Division (DAK)** specified red to be used for its division sign, but black and white were also used. **21. Panzer,** however, generally used white for its insignia.

It should be noted that many tanks did not carry divisional signs. Other units used altered signs when sub-units were attached on a temporary basis. For example, in late 1943, the German Army started the process of issuing the new *Panther* tank to regular armored divisions. One battalion of each regiment (usually, but not always, I battalion) was sent to Germany to receive their vehicles and undergo the special training needed to handle this new tank. Time and circumstances often did not allow these battalions to return directly to their parent divisions. Thus, for much of the period of late 1943-1944, *Panther* battalions often fought with other divisions, whose immediate needs were paramount:

I/Pz Rgt 6 (3. PD) acted as **I/Pz Lehr Regiment (PzLehr Div.)**
I/Pz Rgt 11 (6. PD) acted as **I/Pz Rgt 10 (8. PD)**
I/Pz Rgt "Grossdeutschland" acted as **I/Pz Rgt 11 (6. PD)**

In **Panzer Lehr Division,** the *Panther* battalion, from **3. Panzer Division,** used a larger white outline **"L"** rather than the normal solid **"L"**. Similar alterations may have occurred in other divisions.

Paintings have been included to show, in color, the known (or probable) markings for German *Panzer Divisions*. Note that many of the later divisions did not exist for the whole period of the war; some were formed late, and others were destroyed or disbanded.

1. Panzer Division was formed in several stages, beginning in 1934/35 as a "Panzer Trials Division". **1. Panzer** took part in the occupation of Sudetenland and Czechoslovakia, and by the summer of 1939 was complete with support troops. The division chose as its emblem the white oakleaf, and this was apparently used in the Polish campaign although no photographic record remains. In France, 1940, the oakleaf was widely used and was commonly seen in photos of **1. Panzer Division** vehicles. In the preparation for *Barbarossa* **1. Panzer** was supposed to use a new symbol, a yellow inverted **"Y"**. The division resisted this, painting the new sign primarily on command and leading vehicles but retaining the oakleaf on support vehicles. From 1943-45, the use of the white oakleaf was normal, and this was tolerated by **OKW** and **OKH**.

2. Panzer Division was formed in 1935 in Germany, and with the occupation of Austria in 1938, moved to Vienna where it was garrisoned. **2. Panzer** took part in the Polish campaign, and though there is no photographic evidence, the divisional emblem at this time was a pair of solid yellow circles fairly small—about 25-30 mm diameter. This same symbol was used in France, 1940. For *Barbarossa,* **2. Panzer** adopted the new official sign of an inverted **"Y"** with one tick mark. This was used for most of the 1941-43 period. In 1943, this marking was replaced by a white trident, usually with the center tine longer than the sides. The trident was used for the rest of the war.

A SdKfz 263 of 1. Panzer Division shows the division oakleaf inside the symbol for signals units. The company number (1) is next to this symbol. (Bundesarchiv)

A SdKfz 251 ausf B of the 1. Panzer Division in France, May 1940 shows the division emblem over the tactical sign for the 10th company of motorized infantry. (National Archives)

Photographed in Belgium, May 1940, this pennant denotes a tank battalion in the 1. Panzer Division. The colors are pink—black—pink. The white oakleaf is the division sign, and could be applied to any pennants in the division to identify the units. (National Archives)

This PzKpfw IV ausf A of 1. Panzer Division carries white turret numbers and the *Barbarossa* (1941) division sign. This vehicle was photographed in France in the spring of 1941.

Seen in Russia, this 1. P.D SdKfz 253 artillery observation vehicle carries the yellow division sign and, in white, a tactical sign for the first battery of a towed artillery battalion. (Bundesarchiv)

A SdKfz 253 halftrack of 1. Panzer Division in overall dark gray shows the 1941 inverted "Y" in yellow above a sign for a towed gun battery. This division sign was used primarily during the invasion of Russia, the division later reverting to the white oakleaf. (Bundesarchiv)

A 2. Panzer Division **PzKpfw II ausf C** of the signals platoon of II battalion HQ, photographed near Sedan in 1940. The division's 1939-40 sign, 2 small yellow dots, is in front of the cross. The vehicle designator is in white. Note the breaking of the cross out to the antenna trough. (National Archives)

Temporary Marking 2. Panzer Division, 1939

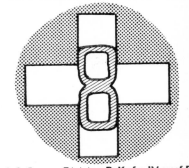

A 2. Panzer Division **PzKpfw IV ausf D** carries new markings. The division dots in yellow, and a black and white cross. The identity of the older painted out sign is not known. "222" is yellow. (Bundesarchiv)

A SdKfz 253 of a towed artillery battalion, 2. Panzer Division, seen in Russia, 1941. The yellow division sign (an inverted "Y" and one bar) was used during the campaigns in Greece and Russia. (Bundesarchiv)

(Above Right) This self-propelled 15 cm heavy infantry gun (sIG 33) on a PzKpfw I chassis was photographed in Greece. *Alter Fritz* (Old Fritz) is in white, as is the tactical sign for a self-propelled gun company. The division sign is yellow. (Bundesarchiv)

This side view of a PzKpfw III ausf F of 2. Panzer Division shows the usual markings for this unit: The use of a rhomboid number plate, the white cross, the division sign in yellow, and the chassis number in white. (Bundesarchiv)

2. Panzer Division PzKpfw IIIs could be distinguished by the large rear stowage boxes, painted with the chassis numbers of the tanks. The yellow division sign (barely visible) is at the lower left corner of the tailplate near the cross. Note the 402 rhomboid plate, partially obscured. (Bundesarchiv)

This group of photos of 6th Company, II battalion, Pz Rgt 3, 2. Panzer Division in Russia, shows an unusual series of markings adopted by the battalion. The rear view of 631 shows the usual divisional markings system: yellow division sign, and a panzer rhomboid and 6 in yellow, denoting the 6th company of the *Panzer Regiment*. 631 is in white. The battalion adopted the motif of a winged serpent with different outlines in white for the different platoons. The color of the serpent may have varied among the platoons, but it appears generally to have been one color, possibly red or green. 602 has a shieldshaped outline, and this was probably used only by 601 and 602. Other geometric shapes used also included the circle and square, but the exact sequence depended on the unit. These are all PzKpfw III ausf J s, and all carry the division sign and rhomboid on their sides also. (Bundesarchiv)

A front view of a PzKpfw IV ausf H shows standard markings, all in white: the trident, vehicle chassis number, and outlined turret numbers. Many 2. PD tanks carried all these markings. (Bundesarchiv)

A rare shot of a SdKfz 234/2 *Puma* armored car; only 101 were produced so they were unusual. This vehicle carries very unobtrusive markings for an armored car company of the reconnaissance battalion of 2. Panzer Division, in white. The trident here is fairly small. Here the breaks caused by the stencils have not been filled in.

This Ford *Maultier* truck shows the division sign, and the increasingly common practice of painting the license plates even on softskin vehicles. Presumably this was to conserve critically needed materials. (Bundesarchiv)

3. Panzer Division was formed in 1935, headquartered in Berlin. **Pz Rgt 6** of this division formed the cadre for the **Pz Lehr Abt** *Legion Kondor*, which, filled with volunteers from all the *Pz Rgts.*, saw service in the Spanish Civil War. During the Polish campaign, **3. Panzer's** emblem was a yellow "E" lying on its side, arms down. This may have been a very stylized depiction of the famous *Brandenburg* Gate in Berlin. Again, no photographic evidence from the Polish campaign has confirmed the use of this symbol. In France and Belgium, 1940, **3. Panzer Division** used the same symbol for its vehicles. For the invasion of Russia, **3. Panzer Division** used the new

"official" sign, an inverted "Y" in yellow with two tick marks. The division, however, continued to use the "Berlin Bear" as a personal emblem. All vehicles in the division could use the bear in a white shield, and the tanks in **Pz Rgt 6** also used a standing bear without a shield. This bear was often painted in different colors, perhaps to indicate the company. Colors used included white, red, yellow, and blue. Part of **3. Panzer** was sent to Libya as a cadre for the **5. Light Division**, which later became **21. Panzer Division**. These vehicles at first still carried the **3. Panzer Division** sign.

This rare photo shows the 1939-40 sign for 3. Panzer Division. This PzKpfw I ausf A has been converted into a workshop recovery vehicle. The "Death's Head" (*Totenkopf*) in white was the symbol of all armor troops. The division sign, in yellow, may be a greatly simplified symbol of the Brandenburg gate in Berlin, the division home station. (National Archives)

This PzKpfw II of 3. Panzer Division **was photographed during the campaign in France. Barely visible is the yellow division sign on the front plate. The turret numbers are large outlines in white, the centers remaining dark gray. This tank is in the 5th company, 4th platoon.**

Divisional Insignia

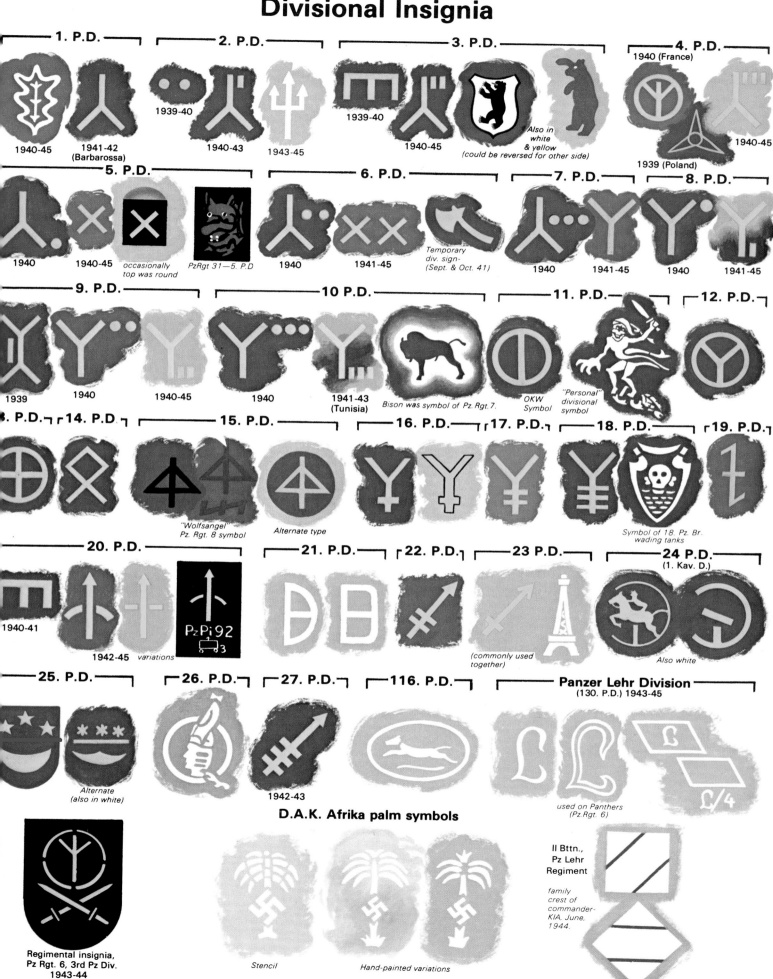

1. P.D.
1940-45 | 1941-42 (Barbarossa)

2. P.D.
1939-40 | 1940-43 | 1943-45

3. P.D.
1939-40 | 1940-45 | Also in white & yellow (could be reversed for other side)

4. P.D.
1940 (France) | 1939 (Poland) | 1940-45

5. P.D.
1940 | 1940-45 | occasionally top was round | PzRgt 31–5. P.D

6. P.D.
1940 | 1941-45 | Temporary div. sign- (Sept. & Oct. 41)

7. P.D.
1940 | 1941-45

8. P.D.
1940 | 1941-45

9. P.D.
1939 | 1940 | 1940-45

10 P.D.
1940 | 1941-43 (Tunisia) | Bison was symbol of Pz.Rgt.7.

11. P.D.
OKW Symbol | "Personal" divisional symbol

12. P.D.

13. P.D.

14. P.D.

15. P.D.
"Wolfsangel" Pz. Rgt. 8 symbol | Alternate type

16. P.D.

17. P.D.

18. P.D.
Symbol of 18. Pz. Br. wading tanks

19. P.D.

20. P.D.
1940-41 | 1942-45 | variations | PzPi92 3

21. P.D.

22. P.D.

23 P.D.
(commonly used together)

24 P.D. (1. Kav. D.)
Also white

25. P.D.
Alternate (also in white)

26. P.D.

27. P.D.
1942-43

116. P.D.

Panzer Lehr Division (130. P.D.) 1943-45
used on Panthers (Pz.Rgt. 6)

Regimental insignia, Pz Rgt. 6, 3rd Pz Div. 1943-44

D.A.K. Afrika palm symbols
Stencil | Hand-painted variations

II Bttn., Pz Lehr Regiment

family crest of commander-KIA, June, 1944.

A PzKpfw III ausf H of 3. Panzer Division, seen in Russia, 1941. These are standard markings for the period. The white outline numbers were usually replaced later by solid numbers in different colors. (Bundesarchiv)

Seen during the Don/Stalingrad campaign, 1942, this Horch ambulance has plain red crosses on dark gray paint, and the 3. Panzer Division emblem, the Berlin bear in black on a white shield. The red cross flag was commonly used by German ambulances. (Bundesarchiv)

In 1943-44, **Panzer Regiment 6** of **3. Panzer Division** adopted a regimental emblem. This consisted of a black shield, flat on top, round on the bottom, with the 1939-40 divisional sign for **4. Panzer Division** and a pair of crossed swords below this. Though not confirmed, a possible explanation for this seemingly misplaced old sign is that this shield represented the award of swords to a Knight's Cross, possibly won by the regimental CO while he was serving with **4. Panzer Division** in France 1940. Many officers and men served with several armored units, and some continued to display emblems of former units. The Knights Cross was the highest decoration, and a symbol based on it would be considered a great honor.

Seen in Russia, 1943/44, this SdKfz 251 ausf D halftrack carries an interesting pennant for Pz Rgt 6. The pennant is black and pink, the colors of the armored troops. The cross at the upper corner is outlined in white and symbolizes the awarding of a Knight's Cross. The other symbol is the old 1939-40 sign for 4. Panzer Division with crossed swords below, in yellow. This might indicate the award of swords to the Knight's Cross, while the recipient (Rgt CO?) served with 4. P D in 1940. (Bundesarchiv)

(Above) This late production PzKpfw IV ausf G of the 3. Panzer Division is very similar to the later ausf H. The vehicle is dark yellow, 124 is yellow, and the shield is black with the 4.P.D sign in yellow. The bear is white, and it appears that the bear was painted in different colors for each company: 1st-white; 2nd-red; 3rd-yellow; 4th-blue. (Bundesarchiv)

(Below) A snow camouflaged PzKpfw IV ausf H of 3.PD in Russia, 1943/44. The markings here look somewhat different because of the greater contrast to the white paint. 221 is in yellow, the cross has a smudged gray (obscured black) center, the regimental shield (hidden by the spaced armor door) is black, and the standing bear is red. The next two tanks are dark yellow, the fourth is white. (Bundesarchiv)

Tactical Symbols
1935-42

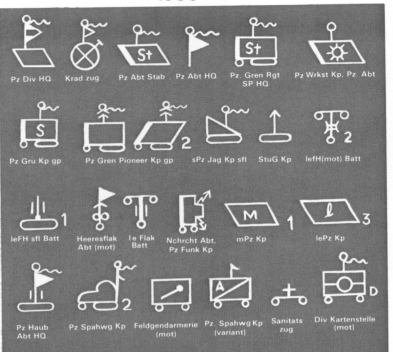

Pz Div HQ	Krad zug	Pz Abt Stab	Pz Abt HQ	Pz Gren Rgt SP HQ	Pz Wrkst Kp, Pz. Abt
Pz Gru Kp gp	Pz Gren Pioneer Kp gp	sPz Jag Kp sfl	StuG Kp	lefH(mot) Batt	
leFH sfl Batt	Heeresflak Abt (mot)	le Flak Batt	Nchrcht Abt, Pz Funk Kp	mPz Kp	lePz Kp
Pz Haub Abt HQ	Pz Spahwg Kp	Feldgendarmerie (mot)	Pz. Spahwg Kp (variant)	Sanitats zug	Div Kartenstelle (mot)

1943-45

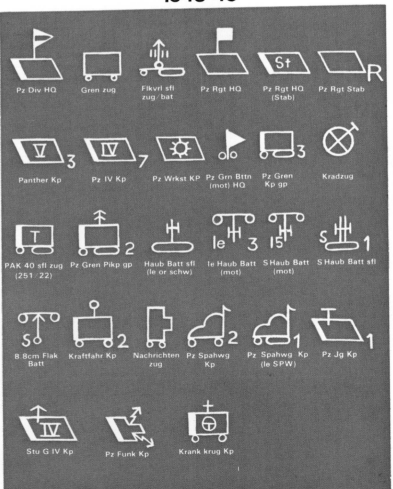

Pz Div HQ	Gren zug	Flkvrl sfl zug / bat	Pz Rgt HQ	Pz Rgt HQ (Stab)	Pz Rgt Stab
Panther Kp	Pz IV Kp	Pz Wrkst KP	Pz Grn Bttn (mot) HQ	Pz Gren Kp gp	Kradzug
PAK 40 sfl zug (251/22)	Pz Gren Pikp gp	Haub Batt sfl (le or schw)	le Haub Batt (mot)	S Haub Batt (mot)	S Haub Batt sfl
8.8cm Flak Batt	Kraftfahr Kp	Nachrichten zug	Pz Spahwg Kp	Pz Spahwg Kp (le SPW)	Pz Jg Kp
Stu G IV Kp	Pz Funk Kp	Krank krug Kp			

National Insignia

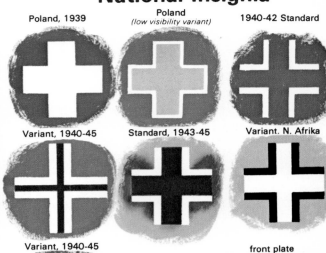

Poland, 1939

Poland (low visibility variant)

1940-42 Standard

Variant, 1940-45

Standard, 1943-45

Variant. N. Afrika

Variant, 1940-45

Variant, 1940-45

License Plates

front plate

WH·1435174

WH 771 431 — Early pattern rear plate

WH 1 254132 — Later pattern rear plate

Command Pennants

Army Group (Armeegruppe)

Army Command (AOK)

Panzer Group (Panzergruppe)

Army Corp (Armeekorp

 Panzer Division

 Panzer Brigade

 Panzer Regiment

 Panzer Batt (Panzer Abte

 Tank destroyer battalion (Pz Jag Abt.)

 Battalion (Aufklarungs Abteilung)

 Battalion (II Abt. / Pz Rgt.)

 Regiment (Panzergrenad

 AFRIKA — Alternate corps pennant (Deutsches Afrikakorps)

 Battalion

Turret Numbers

112 341 115

234 121 33

211 601 42

PzKpfw II ausf C, unit unknown, Prague, 1938

PzKpfw I ausf B, unit unknown, Poland, 1939

PzKpfw I ausf B, unit unknown, Poland, 1939

SdKfz 247 command car, unit unknown, Poland, 1939.

PzKpfw I ausf A, PzKpfw II ausf C and PzKpfw IV ausf B, 5. Panzer Division, Poland, 1939

4. **Panzer** was activated in 1938, and took part in the Polish campaign. Photographic and historical evidence tentatively identifies a three-pointed star as a division symbol for this unit in Poland. In France, several good photographs of **4. Panzer** tanks were taken, and these show the use of a man-rune enclosed within a circle as the divisional sign. In 1941 for the Russian campaign, **4. Panzer** used the inverted "Y" with three tick marks, and used this for the rest of the war. No personal emblem for **4. Panzer Division** is known.

This grim reminder of the costs of war shows an early PzKpfw II destroyed in Warsaw, 1939. This tank has excellent examples of yellow-painted crosses with white borders and yellow numbers. The 3-pointed star has been tentatively identified as the sign of 4. Panzer Division. **(Bundesarchiv)**

This close-up view of an early PzKpfw II of 4. Panzer Division **shows very clearly the design of the stencil. Most PzKpfw IIs with this original round nose plate had applique armor added before the French campaign, giving a square nose glacis plate appearance. (National Archives)**

Photographed in France, 1940, this PzKpfw II carries markings for the signals platoon, I battalion HQ company. The man-rune in a circle, in yellow, was the division's sign, and almost always appears in its unfilled stencilled form. The IN3 and dot are in yellow. Note the white air recognition rectangle painted on the engine deck. **(National Archives)**

This PzKpfw III of 4. Panzer Division, photographed in Flanders or Holland, again shows the division sign and the rear turret number. The exact meaning of the small dot next to the turret number is not known. (National Archives)

1939, Poland

1940, France

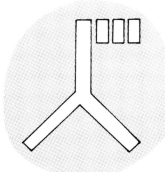

1941-45

4 P.D. Insignia

On the road to St-Pere, France, this PzKpfw II of 4. Panzer Division is part of a long column of vehicles. 216 and dot are in yellow, as is the division sign. Extra stowage carried on this tank is typical of combat vehicles. (National Archives)

PzKpfw II ausf C and PzKpfw I ausf A, PzAbt zbV 40, Norway, 1940.

rear detail

Adler Kfz13 armored car, unit unknown, France, 1940

WH 54653

WH·54653

PzKpfw IV ausf D, 2. Panzer Division, Germany, 1939-40

PzKpfw IV ausf B, 6. Panzer Division, Germany, 1939-40.

This PzKpfw III ausf E of Pz Rgt 31, 5. Panzer Division, was photographed in the Balkans, 1941. The X and 123 are in yellow. The Pz Rgt 31 emblem, the devil's head, is stencilled in red with white teeth and eyes. This emblem was carried only on the tanks in the *Panzer Regiment.* (Bundesarchiv)

PzRgt 31 Devil

This PzKpfw IV ausf F1 of Pz Rgt 31, 5. Pz Div. shows the full range of markings carried by the divisions tanks. This vehicle carries a fresh gloss-painted cross, a black chassis number, the division's yellow X in a red shape, a red 451 on the visor, and a red and white devil's head on a faded black or fresh dark gray background. Strangely enough, this photo indicates very strongly that this color scheme is African brown (RAL 8020) with dark gray (RAL 7027) overspray! (Bundesarchiv)

These Hummels of Pz Art Rgt 116 (armored artillery regiment), 5. Panzer Division, were photographed in 1944. The division X sign (yellow) and the tactical sign for a self-propelled howitzer battery (white) are on one black rectangle. Probably as a result of the 1944 order to renumber these vehicles, 3-digit numbers have replace earlier systems. (Bundesarchiv)

(Below Right) Covered with dust over its African scheme of desert brown paint, this SdKfz 260 radio car of the 2nd company of the signals battalion, 5. Panzer Division, shows a common practice of the division in marking its vehicles: the use of a black rectangle or square as a background for the markings. Some of the old dark gray paint shows on the fenders where the desert brown has worn away. (Bundesarchiv)

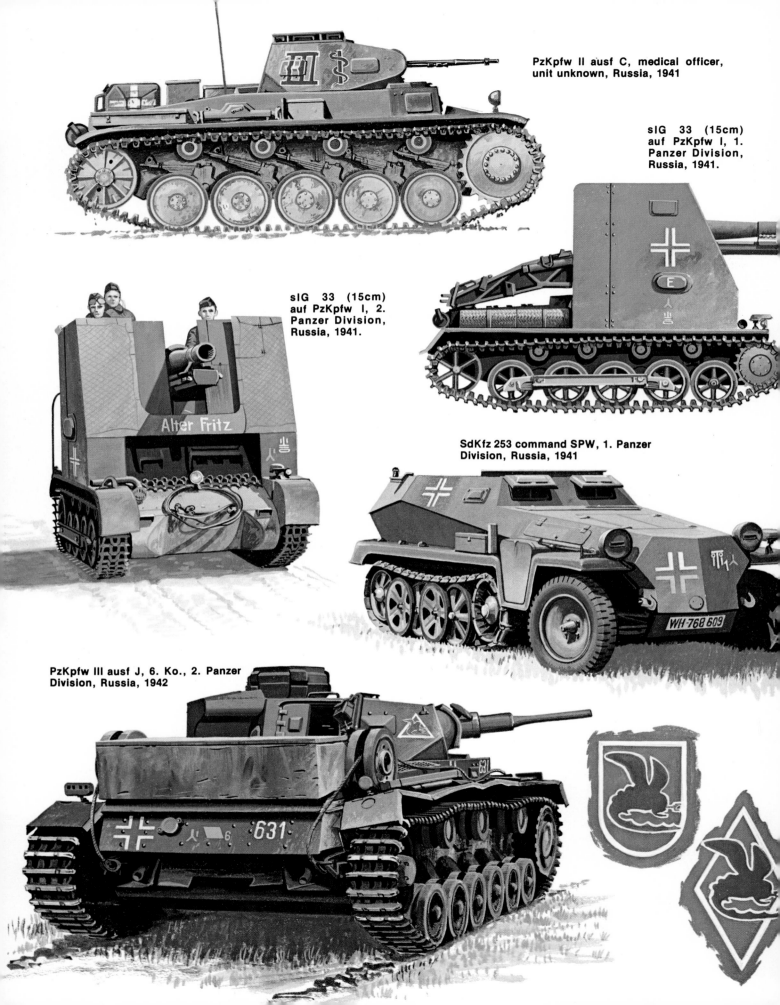

PzKpfw II ausf C, medical officer,
unit unknown, Russia, 1941

sIG 33 (15cm)
auf PzKpfw I, 1.
Panzer Division,
Russia, 1941.

sIG 33 (15cm)
auf PzKpfw I, 2.
Panzer Division,
Russia, 1941.

Alter Fritz

SdKfz 253 command SPW, 1. Panzer
Division, Russia, 1941

WH-768 609

PzKpfw III ausf J, 6. Ko., 2. Panzer
Division, Russia, 1942

631

6. Panzer Division was formed from the **1. Light Division (motorized),** which took part in the Polish campaign. Organized as a full *Panzer Division* in November 1939, **6. Panzer Division** fought in France, 1940. At this time, the division sign was a yellow inverted Y with two round dots. For *Barbarossa,* it adopted the letter symbol of XX in yellow. **6. Panzer Division** attempted the relief of Stalingrad and fought at Kursk. A yellow "war hatchet" was used as a temporary sign, Sept.—Oct. 1941, during the assault on Moscow.

A SdKfz 263 of the reconnaissance battalion of 6. Panzer Division, seen in France. The yellow division sign is just above the right license plate. On the left rear corner of the hull is the tactical sign for the reconnaissance battalion. (Bundesarchiv)

Temporary Marking 6. Panzer Division, 1943

This PzKpfw 35(t) shows the standard 6. Panzer Division markings during the "Phoney War" period, winter 1939-40. The division sign was an inverted Y with two dots, in yellow. At this point, the rhomboid plate was the primary identification of the vehicle. (Bundesarchiv)

A SdKfz 251/4 towing a 10.5 cm light field howitzer in France. The division sign of 6. Panzer Division can be seen to the left of the shovel. The battery tactical sign in white is on the left rear door. The D on the gun is probably the battery identification letter. (Bundesarchiv)

A group of PzKpfw 35(t) light tanks of the 6. Panzer Division shows differences in markings carried. Though all have flags and similar stowage, note that the first tank has only a white outline cross while the second has a black and white cross and the tank number in yellow. (Bundesarchiv)

A Kfz 15 of 6. Panzer Division carries the white tactical sign for a motorized infantry company above the yellow division sign. The front license plate is painted on the fender.

A PzKpfw III ausf E command tank of 6. Panzer Division, probably photographed in Lithuania, 1941. This tank has hand-painted yellow XX insignia, the 1941-45 division sign. The number 103 is in white. (National Archives)

7. Panzer Division was formed in November 1939 from **2. Light Division (mot.)**, and fought in the French campaign as a full *Panzer Division*. Its symbol in France was a yellow inverted "Y" with three dots. Commanded by Erwin Rommel, **7. Panzer Division** fought British armor at Arras and advanced to the English Channel. For *Barbarossa*, **7. Panzer** adopted a new sign, a yellow "Y". The division fought primarily on the Eastern front, but surrendered to U.S. forces in May 1945. The yellow "Y" was used to the end.

Soldiers prepare to ferry this PzKpfw II across a French river. The crosses are black and white, and the division sign, an inverted Y with 3 dots, is in yellow on the hull side. The red and white **11** identifies this vehicle as being in the reconnaissance platooon of a battalion HQ company. This is from 7. Panzer Division **1940**. (Bundesarchiv)

These two views of a PzKpfw II of 7. Panzer Division show the application of many division signs, front and rear. Crosses are black and white, and there is a faded white air recognition band across the engine deck.

This 7. Panzer Division **Ladungsleger I** carries a demolition charge over the engine deck and is in the Pz Pi Abt (armored engineers battalion). It has the open cross and the new 7. Panzer Division sign, adopted in late 1940.

This SdKfz 263 radio vehicle of 7. Panzer Division in Russia displays markings of a division HQ vehicle. The division pennant (black-white-red) is painted on the spaced armor. The division Y sign is yellow, and the signals unit tactical signs (2nd signals company PD HQ battalion) are yellow. (National Archives)

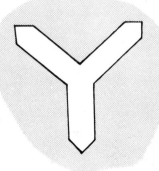

7. Panzer Division Insignia
Variant

The invasion of Russia involved most of the armored units in the German army. Here, a PzKpfw II of the III battalion's HQ reconnaissance platoon is seen in typical 1941 markings. The narrow style crosses are white, the III 14 is red and white, and the division signs are yellow. (Bundesarchiv)

8. Panzer Division was formed in late 1939 from **3. Light Division (mot.).** The division fought in France, 1940, using as a sign a yellow "Y" with one round dot. It was one of the divisions held back from the Dunkirk beachhead by **OKH**. In Russia, 1941, **8. Panzer** used a new sign, a yellow "Y" with one yellow tick mark. This sign was used to the end of the war, **8. Panzer** surrendering in Moravia in May 1945.

This single photograph of 8. Panzer Division **vehicles shows a PzKpfw II and PzKpfw 38(t) of the HQ staff unit of II battalion,** Pz Rgt 10. **The tanks are dark gray, crosses are white, and the II and division sign (a Y with one bar) are yellow. This is the invasion of Russia, 1941.(Bundesarchiv)**

9. Panzer Division was formed from **4. Light Division (mot.),** formed from ex-Austrian Army units. **4. Light Division** fought in Poland. **9. Panzer Division,** activated in late 1939, fought in Holland, 1940, then in France. The division sign then was a yellow "Y" with two round dots. **9. Panzer** went to the Balkans, using the new sign, a yellow "Y" with two tick marks. This was used until the end of the war. One source indicates the **9. Panzer Division** may have used another symbol just after its formation. This was a pair of yellow vertical lines, the right line being a bit longer and having "V" lines at each end, thus resembling an "X" stretched in the middle. This may have been a very stylized depiction of the Roman numeral "IX", but this is not known. At any rate, this marking existed for only a very short period of time.

A Befehlspanzer III and SdKfz 251/3 (or/6) command halftrack of 9. Panzer Division, **seen in Russia, 1941. The division pennant is black-white-red, and the division sign is yellow. The white battalion tactical sign was often used to indicate a divisional headquarters unit. (Bundesarchiv)**

This Zundapp KS 750 motorcycle, seen in Yugoslavia, 1941, carries a rough hand-painted division sign. Many signs were painted by hand when stencils were not available. (Bundesarchiv)

Zundapp

Also seen in Yugoslavia, this SdKfz 251 has the yellow division sign and the white tactical sign for the 1st motorized infantry company. Note the varied uniforms and equipment of the captured Yugoslav soldiers. The fourth man from the left is wearing a prewar Czech helmet. (Bundesarchiv)

10. Panzer Division was formed in the summer of 1939. Its formation was not complete by the start of the Polish campaign, and divisional units fought under other commands. Its armored element, **4. Panzer Brigade** formed **Panzer Verband Ostpreussen** with some 55 units. Completed in time for the French campaign in 1940, **10. Panzer Division** carried the official sign of a yellow "Y" with three round dots. **Pz Rgt 7**, however, had previously adopted the silhouette of a bison as their regimental symbol, and this marking was commonly found on **10. Panzer** tanks. The bison was unusual in that generally a reverse stencil was used: the bison was in the tank

color, with a sprayed border of white (on dark gray) or black (on brown vehicles). **10. Panzer Division** was also noted for its custom of painting only company numbers on the tanks. For *Barbarossa*, **10.Panzer Division** adopted the new official sign of a yellow "Y" with three tick marks. The division was destroyed in Tunisia in 1943. While there, at least a few vehicles had the platoon and vehicle numbers added in smaller figures. This may have resulted from the formation of so many battle groups in Tunisia, with another formation commander insisting on the more complete identification, or simply a change in practice.

A PzKpfw I and staff car of Pz Rgt 7, 10. Panzer Division, **photographed in Russia in the winter of 1941-42. The tank carries the 1941-43 sign of the division in yellow and a white cross. The staff car has a white stencilled rhomboid and R indicating the staff of** Pz Rgt 7, **a yellow divisional sign, and the sprayed outline of** Pz Rgt 7's **bison emblem. (Bundesarchiv)**

PzRgt 7 Bison

10. Panzer Division **was unusual in generally marking only the company numbers on its tank. Here, a PzKpfw III of** Pz Rgt 7 **travels through a burning Russian village, 1941. 7 refers to the 7th company. Barely visible next to this is the outline of the regiment's bison emblem. A chassis number in white is painted above the driver's visor. (Bundesarchiv)**

A SdKfz 251 carries a heavy machine gun section in France, 1942. This 10.PD **APC belongs to the 7th company of a** *Panzergrenadier* (armored infantry) regiment.Many divisions used this tactical sign, for motorized infantry, instead of the armored infantry sign with a halftrack symbol below the rectangle. Note the field post number stamped on the license plate. (Bundesarchiv)

(Above Left) Seen in Tunisia, 1942-43, this PzKpfw III shows the effects of weathering. Note the dust on the upper surfaces. On the turret rear, in black, are the company number, 2, and the bison emblem. The significance of the white circles is not known at this time, but could indicate the 2nd company, as the circle was used by some units to denote the second section (sub-unit) of a regiment, battalion, etc. (Bundesarchiv)

This Sd Kfz 222 armored car of 10. Panzer Division carries the division sign (partly overpainted) and the tactical sign of a motorcycle reconnaissance company, both in yellow. The dark gray on this vehicle seems to be the original gray color of the vehicle, the brown having been oversprayed. (Bundesarchiv)

Providing an interesting contrast in colors, these SdKfz 250s of 10. Panzer Division were photographed in Tunisia. Because of shortages of paint, the vehicle on the left has been painted in the new dark yellow paint, the right hand 250 is in the desert brown shade, which is darker. The right vehicle is from the headquarters of the 1st artillery battalion of the artillery regiment. The left vehicle is from the 2nd battery of the battalion. Division signs are yellow. (Bundesarchiv)

This well-known shot of a 10. Panzer Division PzKpfw IV ausf G shows an unusual set of markings carried in the later stages of the Tunisian campaign, 1943. At this time, many 10. PD tanks carried no markings except for the crosses. This tank originally displayed only the company number, 8, in black. 23 (3rd tank, 2nd platoon) was added later in white. There were several dozen battle groups in Tunisia and marking changes were not uncommon. (Bundesarchiv)

15. Panzer Division was formed in late 1940, and in April 1941 was sent to Africa as part of the **Deutsches Afrikakorps (DAK).** The divisional sign was a triangle divided by a vertical bar, usually painted in red, black, or sometimes white. **Pz Rgt 8** of this division had a regimental symbol, a *wolfsangel* (wolf-trap), usually painted in red. As part of the **DAK**, all **15. Panzer** vehicles could carry the white palm tree insignia of this corps.

15. Panzer Division also usually painted only the company numbers on its tanks in Africa. Most common were red numbers, but black, sometimes outlined in white, also were seen. A system of playing card symbols was used by **Pz Rgt 8** in Tunisia, but regrettably no record or memory of this has survived, so far as is known.

This PzKpfw III ausf J has the later darker brown scheme. The company number, 6, is red, as are the division sign near it, and 632 below. 632 is the full designation for this tank, but most Pz Rgt 8 vehicles did not display the full number. (Bundesarchiv)

Totenkopf
Death's Head)

A PzKpfw II of the 8th company, II battalion, Pz Rgt 8, 15. Panzer Division, in Libya, 1941. 8 is black and white, the division sign is red, and the DAK palm trees are white. Overall vehicle color is yellow-brown. (Bundesarchiv)

A command tank (PzKpfw III) of I battalion, Pz Rgt 8, displays an interesting variant of the 15. PD sign: the symbol is in the vehicle color, but the surrounding circular field is red. I is also red, on a yellow-brown vehicle. (Bundesarchiv)

DAK Palm

Regrettably only a partial view, this photo of a PzKpfw III stowage bin shows most of the markings carried by tanks of Pz Rgt 8, 15. Panzer Division. 1 is black and white, the palm tree is white, and the 15. PD sign and Pz Rgt 8 emblem (a wolfsangel) are in red. (Bundesarchiv)

16. Panzer Division was formed in late 1940, and received as a symbol a yellow "Y" with one bar across the shaft. **16. Panzer Division** fought in the East until destroyed at Stalingrad. A new division was formed in France in the spring of 1943, receiving the same symbol. The sign was often outlined in black, possibly marking the loss of the first formation, but more likely to provide contrast between the dark yellow paint of the vehicles and the yellow used for the symbols. **16. Panzer** served in Italy, then returned to the Eastern front in late 1943-44.

This SdKfz 250 has 3 color schemes! Originally painted dark gray, it was repainted dark yellow but with areas of gray masked off around the markings. On top of this, a coat of winter white paint has been applied. The markings, all in yellow, denote the 4th company, 16th reconnaissance battalion, 16. Panzer Division. **(Bundesarchiv)**

A column of APCs of 16. Panzer Division, showing the use of red division sign and tactical marking on the white paint. The tactical sign denotes the 6th company of Panzergrenadier Regiment 64. **(Bundesarchiv)**

A PzKpfw IV ausf G of 16. Panzer Division, seen in Italy, 1943. This is from the reformed (second) 16. PD. Overall color is dark yellow, turret numbers are black stencilled outlines. The yellow division sign is outlined in black for better contrast against the dark yellow paint. **(Bundesarchiv)**

17. Panzer Division was formed in the fall of 1940. The division fought almost entirely on the Eastern front. The divisional sign was a yellow "Y" with two bars across the shaft.

18. Panzer Division was formed in October 1940, and was initially equipped with the deep-wading tanks (Tauch Pz Kpfw) originally developed for the invasion of England. The division used as a sign a yellow "Y" with three bars across its shaft. The wading tanks of **Panzer Brigade 18** used a special emblem: a shield edged in white, containing a white skull and lines of water in white. This was not a divisional emblem. **18. Panzer Division** was disbanded late in 1943, and was reorganized as an artillery division. Records indicate that the **18. Artillery Division** continued using the same sign.

19. Panzer Division was formed in October 1940. Because this division was largely recruited from lower Saxony, an area noted for its great forests, it adopted as its divisional symbol a yellow *wolfsangel* (wolf-trap). The *wolfsangel* was a very old device long used by hunters and foresters. The **19. Panzer Division** served primarily in the East, but did see service during the 1944 Warsaw uprising. It should be noted that several German formations adopted the *wolfsangel* as a symbol.

This **Horch Kfz 15** car of a PK (propaganda company) attached to 19. Panzer Division shows the use of civilian license plates, common with PK vehicles. The WH refers to *Wehrmacht Heere* **(Army.)** The division sign is white. (Bundesarchiv)

20. Panzer Division was formed in October 1940. At first, its symbol was a yellow "E" on its side, arms down, identical to the earlier **3. Panzer Division** sign. In 1943 or early 1944, **20. Panzer** received a new sign: a yellow arrow breaking through a curved barrier (borderline). A variation of this sign was the use of a straight line. Some signs had colors added, and at least a few had the arrow pointing obliquely down to the right. Stencils allowed some variety in application.

This photo of two destroyed tanks of 20. Panzer Division **in Russia show enigmatic markings which do not follow the standard practices. All markings are in yellow. The PzKpfw 38(t) has a 20. PD sign and a 6 indicating the 6th company, II battalion. The PzKpfw IV ausf D carries non-standard numbers whose meaning is not known. It is unlikely that either 60 or 66 refers to the 6th company since normally PzKpfw IVs and PzKpfw 38(t)s did not belong in the same company. However, equipment shortages could have made this necessary.** (Bundesarchiv)

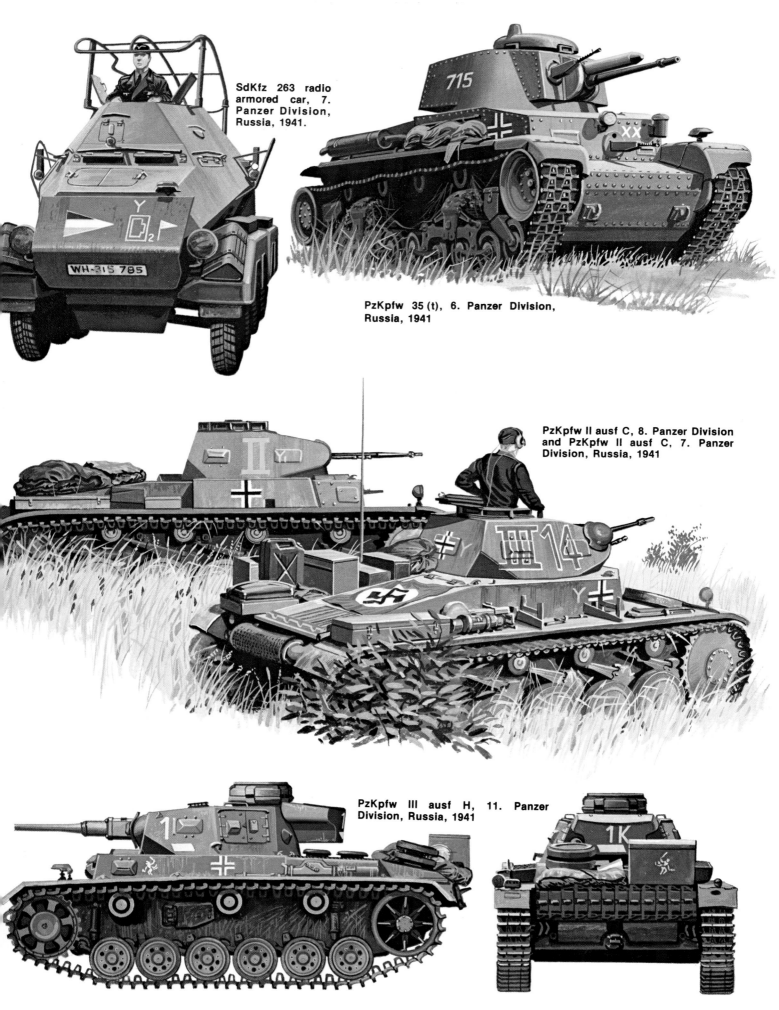

SdKfz 263 radio armored car, 7. Panzer Division, Russia, 1941.

PzKpfw 35 (t), 6. Panzer Division, Russia, 1941

PzKpfw II ausf C, 8. Panzer Division and PzKpfw II ausf C, 7. Panzer Division, Russia, 1941

PzKpfw III ausf H, 11. Panzer Division, Russia, 1941

Photographed in Russia, this PzKpfw 38(t) of 20. Panzer Division carries the early division sign, identical to the old 3. PD symbol. The sign is yellow, as is the turret number. 9 refers to the 9th company, III battalion, Pz Rgt 21. (Bundesarchiv)

A SdKfz 222 armored car, seen in Russia, 1943. This vehicle carries the new division sign for 20. Panzer Division in yellow, an arrow breaking through a curved line, representing a border boundary. The yellow tactical sign is for the 1st motorcycle company of the reconnaissance battalion. The box on the front bumper carries spares for the 2cm KwK 38 main gun, and is so marked in white. An illegible vehicle name is on the turret side. (Bundesarchiv)

This fine view of a SdKfz 251/7 ausf D engineers' APC shows the method used by several divisions to make the tactical signs more visible: a black rectangle as a background. Here the division sign is in yellow. Below it is Pz Pi 92 (armored engineers' battalion 92) in white, below this, the white tactical sign for an engineer company, with the number 3. The white 3 is repeated larger near the sign and 302 refers to the AD's vehicle in the 3rd company.

21. Panzer Division was actually two divisions. The "first" **21. Panzer Division** was formed in the summer of 1941 from the **5. Light Division,** itself drawn largely from **3. Panzer Division. 21.Panzer Division** formed part of the **DAK,** and all vehicles usually carried the **DAK** palm tree sign as well as the white "D" split by a horizontal line. This was sometimes almost a rectangle rather than a "D"—many of these signs were hand-painted. This "first" **21. Panzer Division** was destroyed in Tunisia with all other German forces in Africa.

The "second" **21. Panzer Division** was formed in France in the summer of 1943, using French tanks. It fought on the Western front until early 1945, when it was destroyed in the East. The "second" formation also used the "D" split by the bar, either in white (usual) or in yellow, but there was no connection between the two units that used this sign and division number.

A captured South African Marmon-Harrington armored car, repainted in 21. Panzer Division markings. The paint scheme seems to be in very bad shape, but it is more likely that a heavy coat of dust has been partically washed away by a rain shower. This vehicle, seen in Tunisia, has the tactical sign for the 4th battery of the artillery regiment. Note the square form of the division sign. (Bundesarchiv)

The first German forces in North Africa were drawn from Pz Rgt 5, 3. Panzer Division. Organized as the 5. Light Division, this unit was later reformed as the 21. Panzer Division. Here are PzKpfw Is, IIs and IVs carrying their European color scheme, dark gray with white outline numbers. Even later, 21. PD tanks commonly had white outline turret numbers.

A SdKfz 263 radio vehicle of 5. Light Division. No special sign was issued for this unit, and since most of its troops had come from 3. Panzer Division, the vehicles generally used the yellow inverted Y and 2 bars of that division. This vehicle, camouflaged with mud, displays this old sign. (Bundesarchiv)

PzKpfw II ausf D, 14. Panzer Division, Russia, 1941.

PzKpfw 38(t), 20. Panzer Division, Russia, 1941.

Zundapp KS600 combination, 14. Panzer Division, Russia, 1942

SdKfz 251/c SPW, 22. Panzer Division, Russia, 1942

SdKfz 261 radio armored car, 24. Panzer Division, Russia, 1942-43

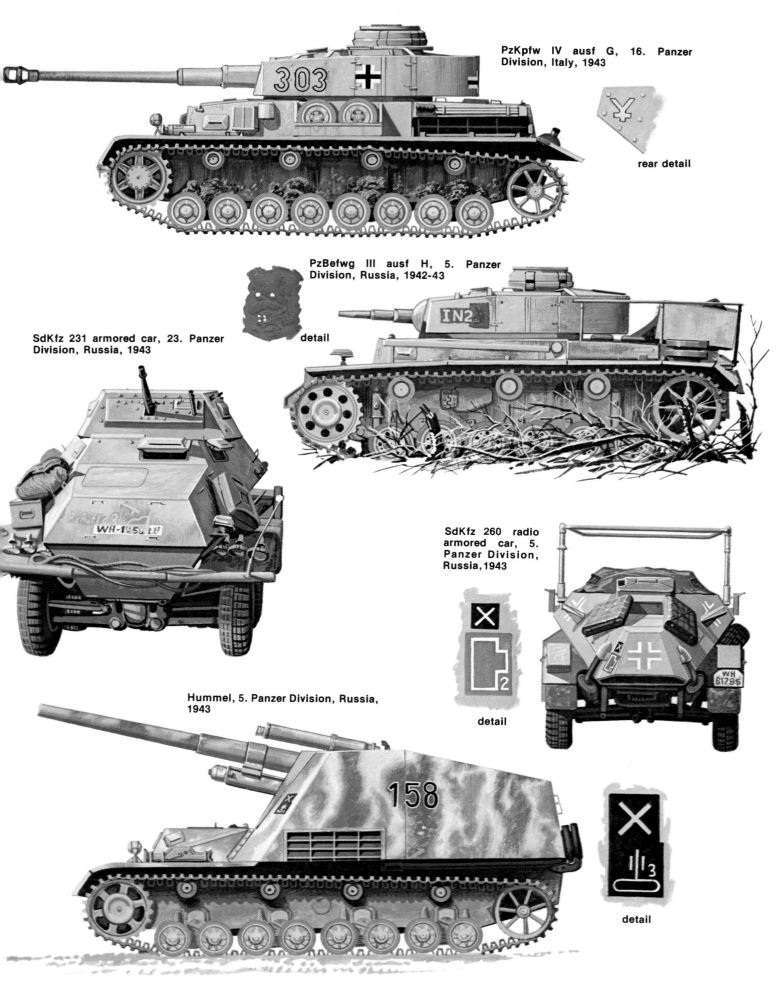

PzKpfw IV ausf G, 16. Panzer Division, Italy, 1943

rear detail

PzBefwg III ausf H, 5. Panzer Division, Russia, 1942-43

detail

SdKfz 231 armored car, 23. Panzer Division, Russia, 1943

SdKfz 260 radio armored car, 5. Panzer Division, Russia, 1943

detail

Hummel, 5. Panzer Division, Russia, 1943

detail

24. Panzer Division was reorganized in the winter of 1941-42 from the old **1. Kavallerie Division.** As a result, **24. Panzer** retained the old "leaping horse and rider" symbol used by the **1. Kavallerie. 24. Panzer** fought in the east until destroyed at Stalingrad. A new **24. Panzer Division** was reformed in France in April 1943, serving in Italy, then the Eastern front again. This second formation officially was to use a simpler sign in which the "leaping horse and rider" was replaced by a simple bar (sometimes a "panzer" rhomboid) leaping a barrier in the open circle. It appears, however, that the use of the old cavalry sign may have continued, to keep the division's history and traditions, and even today, the veterans of the **24. Panzer Division** use the horse and rider sign, though the division's war memorial uses the simpler "official" second sign. Photos of the **24. Panzer** vehicles show that white was used nearly as often as yellow for painting the division symbols.

Here, a PzKpfw III ausf J of 24. Panzer Division is unloaded from a flatcar in Russia. The division sign, from the old 1. Kavallerie Division, is on the right front mudguard flap in white. On the front plate, note the plain yellow arrow. This might have been the officially assigned OKW division sign for the 24. PD which would be in sequence with the signs of the previous two divisions. But if so, the unit did not adopt it, and it does not appear again. The chassis number is white, as is the turret number, 532. The MG cover is from another tank. (Bundesarchiv)

The 24. Panzer Division sign on this BMW R75 with sidecar is painted in yellow. It was applied by brush through stencil. (Bundesarchiv)

It was common practice to mask off markings when repainting a vehicle, as on this SdKfz 260, which has been fitted with an MG mount from an APC. The division sign and signals company tactical sign are yellow.

Later 24.PD Insignia

Vehicles of the 24. Panzer Division advancing in Russia, during the Don campaign in 1942. The division signs are applied in yellow, but the turret numbers on the tanks are white. Some division signs were also white. The tactical sign on the SdKfz 251/3 at right is in yellow. (Bundesarchiv)

25. Panzer Division was activated in the summer of 1943 in France. It served mainly on the Eastern front, but managed at the end to retreat to the West, and surrender to U.S. forces in Germany. This division apparently had two signs, but the more complex one probably was not used. It was a round-bottomed red shield divided by a black horizontal line, with three yellow stars above, and a yellow crescent below the line. The more likely vehicle sign was a stencil showing a row of three stars over a horizontal line over a modified crescent. This was generally applied in white or yellow, though black and red were often used over white winter camouflage schemes by many units.

26. Panzer Division was formed in October 1943 in France,

and adopted as a symbol a rather complex stencil of a Prussian grenadier's head in a circle—this was usually painted in white. The **26.** fought in Italy until the German surrender in May 1945, the last Army *Panzer Division* in Italy.

27. Panzer Division was formed in September 1942 in the Ukraine, from units drawn partly from **22. Panzer Division**. The division sign was a yellow arrow with three bars across the shaft, very similar to that of the **22. Panzer Division**, an arrow with two bars. Never existing as a full-fledged *Panzer Division*, the **27.** was disbanded, along with its "parent" **22.Panzer Division,** following very heavy losses in the Stalingrad campaign, early 1943. Neither was reformed.

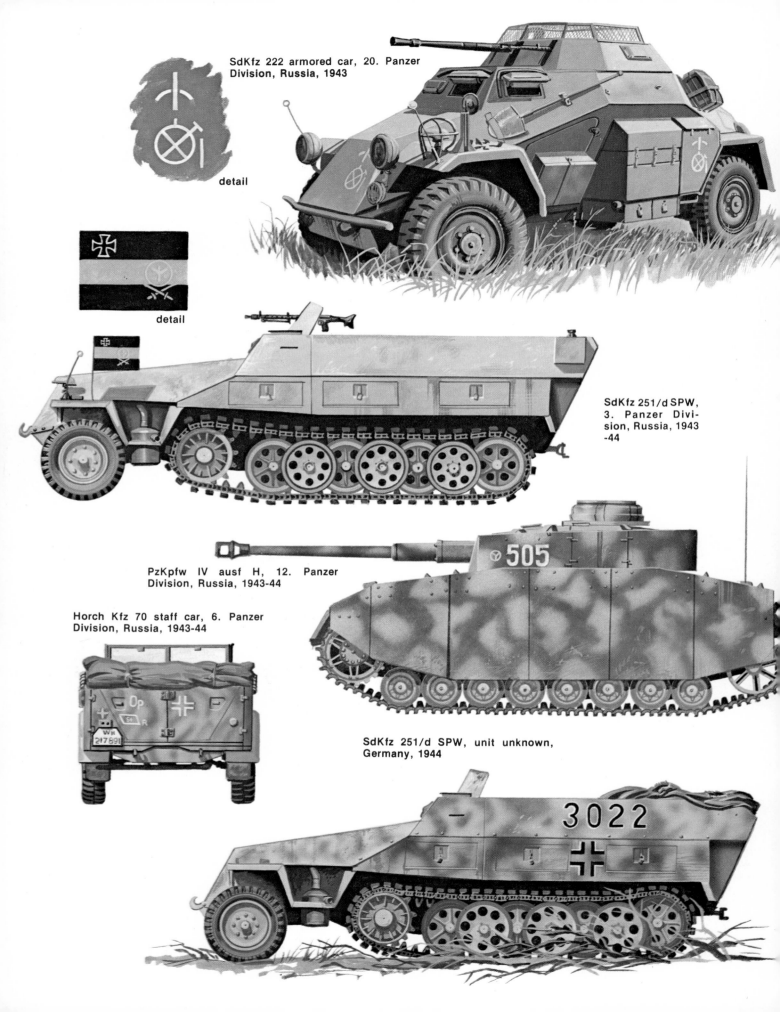

SdKfz 222 armored car, 20. Panzer
Division, Russia, 1943

detail

detail

SdKfz 251/d SPW,
3. Panzer Divi-
sion, Russia, 1943
-44

PzKpfw IV ausf H, 12. Panzer
Division, Russia, 1943-44

Horch Kfz 70 staff car, 6. Panzer
Division, Russia, 1943-44

505

SdKfz 251/d SPW, unit unknown,
Germany, 1944

3022

These armored cars of 24. Panzer Division show a very unusual variation of the Army license plates. Here, the plates are dark gray and the numbers white. As these plates were painted with stencils, various colors were possible, though quite rare. (Bundesarchiv)

This fine closeup of a Kfz 15 car of 11. Panzer Division shows the division's personal emblem over the front license plate. Note that this plate has been painted on the fender; this was common on these cars. Note the *Feldpostnummer* (Field Post Number) stamped on the plate for unit identification. The French helmet was from the Yugoslav army which purchased much French equipment before the war. (Bundesarchiv)

An ex-British Bedford truck captured in France, 1940, serves new masters. This vehicle has received standard Army license plates, with a field post number stamped after the WH. The shield is probably from the German transport unit. (National Archives)

Service Markings

In common with most vehicles, German military equipment was often marked with various servicing instructions, data plates and labels, chassis numbers, etc. While most vehicles had a full complement of such markings at the factory, field repainting and camouflage schemes often obliterated much of this. Some markings were reapplied after painting, but many were not, and it was not unusual to see German vehicles devoid of all service markings.

There were several categories of service markings, applied to different classes of vehicles. The most common and prominent on new vehicles was the railroad loading label. This was a painted (stencilled) data plate which in its full form gave the vehicle's designation (*Kfz* or *SdKfz* number), loaded and/or net weight in tonnes, and the loading class code for railroad shipments. It varied quite a bit in size, from small 8" x 10" (20 cm x 25 cm) outlines to large panels that covered the better part of doors on truck cabs. Often the manufacturers prepared the stencils generally used to apply these markings. Many of these were screen-type stencils, which resulted in clean, unbroken letters. Usually the labels were smaller on armored vehicles, and on some tanks, notable the *PzKpfw IV* and *Panther*, the marking was a small rectangle which contained only the *SdKfz* number and weight class code, or often only the letter. Shipping classes were determined by weight and size. Heavy vehicles, such as the *Tiger* tank, required special transport cars and were handled as separate cases. So far the use of railroad load class labels on *Tiger Is* and *Tiger IIs* has not been confirmed. They are not visible in available photographs.

A second type of service marking was the tire pressure notation, carried on fenders and mudguards of wheeled vehicles, directly above the tires. Many of these stencilled markings were overpainted, but some units did replace them after camouflaging their vehicles. The German tire pressure markings were expressed in "atmospheres", abbreviated *atu*. An atmosphere at sea level is equal to 14.7 psi or one dyne/cm2.

Several other types of service markings were used, but not all appeared on all types of vehicles. The first group consisted of servicing instructions, such as the location of filling points for fuel, oil, or water, especially where these had to be reached through access panels. The *NSU Kettenkrad* carried a good example of these markings, as these oil and coolant fillers were inside the rear body. Some *Kettenkrads* also carried stencilled instructions on checking the adjustment and care of the tracks and roadwheels. A second class of markings were the stowage labels used to identify equipment or tools carried in brackets on vehicles. On new vehicles, some outer brackets were marked, but these usually did not last very long. Almost all internal stowage brackets in tanks and self-propelled guns were marked with stencilled or silk-screened labels. A well equipped medium tank might have several dozen labels, many of which can be seen in photos on vehicle interiors. Many German vehicles had their chassis numbers painted on the superstructure exterior, and this marking was commonly found on new vehicles, though in combat units it was not nearly as prevalent. As each vehicle had manufacturer's stamps and data plates, the painted chassis number was not really necessary and was often overpainted. Other vehicles had their chassis weight in kilograms painted on the superstructure.

The necessity of operating much military traffic at night, for security or safety, led to the danger of serious accidents. As virtually all German military vehicles in the early war period were dark gray, they proved to be very difficult to see at night, especially in blackout conditions. As a result, German units adopted the use of white width markings on dark gray vehicles. These were generally confined to softskins and halftracks, as the white compromised the camouflage effect on combat vehicles. The markings took various forms, but in general consisted of white outlines or borders on fenders, mudguards, and body corners. They were intended to enable other drivers and military traffic police and soldiers to see the vehicles and avoid accidents. These white markings were quite successful, and in many areas of Europe, the white bands were also applied to roadside obstructions — trees, fences, gateposts, etc.— to improve visibility at night or in blackouts. The change to dark yellow paint early in 1943 reduced the use of white blackout markings, but did not eliminate it entirely, as blackouts became more common later in the war. Other markings used for similar purposes include red and white "stop" discs and written instructions to allow certain spacings between vehicles (ie: *Abstand 100m*).

These PzKpfw IVs ausf G seen in Greece, 1943, show the standard load label used for these vehicles. The data lines are reduced to vehicle designation (SdKfz 161), gross weight (23t), and load class for rail shipment (S). (Bundesarchiv)

As can be seen, the size of the loading label was adjusted to fit the space available. This VW *Schwimmwagen* carries a full data plate: Kfz K2s; empty weight—0.83T; payload—0.45T; load class—II. Note the use of narrow *Kubelwagen* wheels and tires.

A **Kfz 15 of** 7. Panzer Division **carries the most common front width marking, a white border on the front fenders and the ends of the front bumper. The division sign is yellow.** (Bundesarchiv)

(Above Right) This Kfz 15 staff car of 1. Panzer Division **carries the tactical sign for a Panzer Regiment staff vehicle and the division oakleaf. Note the white width border on the rear body, and the contrast with the dark gray paint which was hard to see at night. (National Archives)**

This car being used by a propaganda unit carries a civilian license plate, indicating an impressed vehicle. The WH indicates *Wehrmacht Heere* (**Army**). The license code, 1A, is from Berlin. The white circles on the fender are a form of width marking for night traffic control. (Bundesarchiv)

Late convoy marking

Abstand 100m

This heavy truck of the German railroad system has the front width markings in white. The front vertical posts were used to judge width clearances. The license plate has a DR prefix. The raised triangular plate on the cab roof indicates that the truck is towing a trailer. (Bundesarchiv)

Victory Markings

A widespread practice in German military units was the painting of "victory" or "kill" markings on guns or vehicles that had destroyed enemy aircraft, vehicles, or other targets, i.e: buildings, bridges, trains, even a ship sunk by a tank!

Victory markings usually took one of two forms: rings painted around the barrel of the gun, or silhouettes or symbols depicting the targets destroyed. A combination of these two systems was found, in two variations. More commonly, a gun shield would have a silhouette of a target with tick marks (bars) to indicate the number of similar targets destroyed. In fewer cases, the gun barrel rings would have the target silhouettes next to them to indicate the targets hit. Many weapons were used against a variety of targets, and thus several silhouettes—each with its total of kill rings— could be painted on the barrel.

Barrel rings were usually painted in a contrasting color, most often white on a dark gray gun , and black, red, or white on the desert brown and dark yellow used later in the war. Some weapons do have barrel rings in different colors (white and red, white and black), and in some units, this may have indicated different targets or areas of operations (tanks and aircraft, Russian front, Western front, etc.). These were unit practices and not official High Command policy. On some weapons, each barrel band was marked in small labels with the date and type of target destroyed. More unusual was the painting of a small target silhouette inside each band for the same purpose.

Some guns saw a great deal of service and scored many hits. Occasionally, there were so many barrel rings that it was difficult to count them accurately or to find room to paint more. In such cases, the rings were often overpainted, using somewhat wider rings to mark off every five or ten kills. Sometimes the number was painted in the ring, and other times only a total at the end of the wide rings (usually an even number-–50, 75, 85, etc.). Additional kills were painted on individually, and periodically more wide rings would be added as space required. Often, alternating wide rings were painted in contrasting colors--usually black and white. On other weapons, every 5th o ' 10th victory ring was painted in a different color to make counting easier. In any case, these were choices made by the local tank or artillery units or crews. For the most part, the German High Command wanted obvious victory markings subdued or removed to avoid drawing attention to superior crews. Orders to this effect were generally ignored, and victory markings were used throughout the war by towed and self-propelled weapons crews.

This light infantry gun (le I G 18) receives a kill marking for a tank destroyed. Considering that the "can" resting on the barrel casing is the cartridge case, the destroyed vehicle was most probably a light tank. The crewman is applying a bar for this victory. (Bundesarchiv)

This remarkably successful gun crew has marked their 8.8 cm gun with a variety of symbols to separate the categories of targets destroyed: aircraft, tanks, and bunkers. These markings were usually in white on dark gray weapons. The box below the barrel contains the panoramic sight for the gun, used for ground targets. (Bundesarchiv)

This self-propelled PAK 40 on a PzKpfw 38(t) chassis carries barrel rings for victory marks. The silhouettes on the shield show enemy guns destroyed, 3 artillery pieces and one antitank gun. The barrel rings indicate tanks destroyed. (Bundesarchiv)

These two photos of victory markings on 8.8 cm antiaircraft guns show the most common marking, the barrel ring. Here silhouettes of aircraft are used to indicate the targets destroyed. The upper photo is of a Flak 18, the lower one is of a later Flak 37 gun. (Bundesarchiv)

Command and Rank Pennants

Staff vehicles of German commands and personal or official vehicles of commanders were authorized to display pennants or plates denoting the level of command or the officer's rank. These normally were painted metal plates, either square, rectangular or triangular in shape. A coded system of colors and patterns was used with the basic pennant shape to indicate the unit's identity and command level. For major army commands, the pennants were square plates, using red, white, and black. Army corps were represented by a red, white, and black rectangular plate. Divisions were represented by a triangular flag, black over white over red. Pennants for brigades, regiments, and battalions used the *Waffenfarbe* (Arm of Service colors) to indicate the unit within a division. Thus, the Panzer units in a division had black and pink pennants. Often the divisional sign was painted on these command pennants. Brigades had triangular pennants, regiments rectangular plates, and battalions triangular pennants with patterns different from brigade pennants. Reduced size copies of these command plates or pennants were often carried on the front and rear of command vehicles, generally near the license plates. They were painted metal plates on softskins, but were frequently painted directly on the armor of command AFVs.

Rank pennants were authorized for generals, officers, and officials who held officer rank. Prior to 23 April 1941, there was only one pennant for generals and officers, a 20 cm x 30 cm triangular plate. On the above date, two new pennants were added. A second triangular pennant was authorized for generals. It had a gold eagle and swastika in place of the white one of the older pennant, and a more elaborate border. The older pennant was retained for officers and officials. The second new rank pennant was a square plate, 30 cm x 30 cm, introduced for Field Marshals. It featured crossed batons, a different eagle motif, and a dark gray border.

Command pennants were normally carried on the left side of vehicles, the rank pennants on the right when an officer authorized to have such pennants was in his vehicle. When the officer was not in the vehicle, the pennants were to be removed or covered. Special cloth covers were provided to cover the pennants when necessary, and the driver was to cover and uncover the plates as needed.

This division command staff car in Russia carries a division pennant and the earlier general's rank pennant used until April 1941. Most of these pennants were carried in metal frames, and many of the rank pennants were cloth. (Bundesarchiv)

Early Officers Pennant

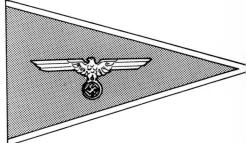

A driver covers the command pennant on this staff car in accordance with the rule requiring such pennants to be covered when the staff officer was not in the vehicles. This is a corps pennant, black-white-red. (Bundesarchiv)

A kl Befehlspanzer I of an unidentified *Panzer Regiment* in the Balkans passes the command flag of an Army Command (AOK). R04 is a regimental staff vehicle, usually the ordnance officer's vehicle. (Bundesarchiv)

This Mercedes staff car carries a division pennant, black-white-red, and the later general's rank pennant, introduced in April 1941. The older general's pennant was then used for field grade officers and officials of equivalent rank. (Bundesarchiv)

The *Kommandeurwagen* displays the rank and command flags for Field Marshal von Kluge. The near pennant is the command flag for an Army High Command (AOK) and the far pennant is the rank flag for Field Marshals introduced in April 1941. (Bundesarchiv)

Field Marshal's Flag

Vehicle Names

The practice of naming individual vehicles was not as widespread in the German Army as it was in the American and British forces. Nonetheless, it was not uncommon, and many German vehicles did carry names. Though many vehicle names were made up by the crews for various reasons (names of wives, sweethearts, characters from literature, cartoons, movies, etc.) many names were chosen in series suggested by unit commanders for reasons of morale or identification.

Early in the war, it was common practice in reconnaissance units to give names to the armored cars. The most common system was to name each vehicle after a city, province, or geographical region of the German Reich. Some armored cars were named after animals. In particular, the great cats were popular subjects and many units used: *Löwe* (Lion), *Panther*, *Tiger*, *Puma*, etc. Assault guns and self-propelled artillery units also used names on occasion, the names generally being in a series within the unit. Supplemental markings were sometimes used, but most often the use of individual vehicle names superseded the use of numbers or letters and was often officially sanctioned.

(Above Left) The name "Margret" on this Panther ausf A seen in Russia is no doubt for the wife or girl of a crew member. Often the tank commander chose the name, but in some crews, the name used might be selected from several suggestions, by lot. (Bundesarchiv)

Though not a vehicle name, this memorial plate to a dead crewman was another personal marking. This marking commemorates the death of a crewman in the 1940 French campaign.

Gerti, a SdKfz 251 ausf D seen in Russia, has an artistically applied name. Again, this vehicle was named after a girl-friend or wife of a crew member. Note the underside details of the 28cm rocket launcher racks. (Bundesarchiv)

Award Shields and Crests

Some German military campaigns involved great sacrifices and demanded extraordinary efforts from combat troops to achieve victory against heavy opposition. In situations in which German units or field commands had distinguished themselves in combat, the High Command **(OKW)** authorized the awarding of campaign crests, shields, and occasionally uniform cuff titles, for some theatres of operations. Though generally limited to command and staff vehicles, such award crests could be painted on vehicles in units which received the award. Two shields confirmed in photos were for service in the Kuban region of Russia and the Crimean peninsula *(Krim)*. Other shields and crests may have been awarded for major battles and campaigns, but the number and names are not known at present.

This VW *Schwimmwagen* **of Army Command (AOK) 17 carries the command pennant, the later general's rank pennant, and a painted crest signifying distinguished service during the Kuban campaign in Russia. (Bundesarchiv)**

A rear shot of the same vehicle, showing the *Kuban* **shield, AOK 17 notation, and a rear command flag for the Army Command. The colors of the shield are not known, but the AOK 17 is white and the painted symbol is probably red. (Bundesarchiv)**